Baedeker's

COLOGNE

W0013558

Imprint

Cover picture: Bank of the Rhine, with the Cathedral and Great St Martin's Church

82 colour photographs
17 ground plans, 6 graphic representations, 2 special plans, 1 transport plan, 1 city plan

Conception and editorial work:
Redaktionsbüro Harenberg, Schwerte
English language: Alec Court

Text:
Thomas Corzelius, Cologne

General direction:
Dr Peter Baumgarten, Baedeker Stuttgart

Cartography:
Ingenieurbüro für Kartographie Huber & Oberländer, Munich
Mairs Geographischer Verlag GmbH & Co., Ostfildern-Kemnat (city plan)

Source of illustrations:
Archiv (1), Corzelius (72), dpa (1), Historia-Photo (3), Holcomb (1), Koch (1), Verkehrsamt (2), ZEFA (1)

English translation:
James Hogarth

Following the tradition established by Karl Baedeker in 1844, sights of particular interest and hotels of particular quality are distinguished by either one or two asterisks.

To make it easier to locate the various sights listed in the "A to Z" section of the Guide, their coordinates on the large city plan (and on the smaller inset plan of the city centre) are shown in red at the head of each entry.

Only a selection of hotels and restaurants can be given: no reflection is implied, therefore, on establishments not included.

In a time of rapid change it is difficult to ensure that all the information given is entirely accurate and up to date, and the possibility of error can never be completely eliminated. Although the publishers can accept no responsibility for inaccuracies and omissions, they are always grateful for corrections and suggestions for improvement.

Contents

Useful Telephone Numbers

Emergencies
  Police | 1 10
  Fire | 1 12
  Ambulance | 74 92 1, 74 50 51
  First aid (Red Cross) | 73 80 21
  Medical emergency service | 72 07 72
  Chemists – out-of-hours service | 11 50
  Breakdown assistance (ADAC – Allgemeiner Deutscher | 37 99 13
  Automobil-Club)

Information
  Tourist Office | 2 21 33 45
  Central Station | 27 61
  Flight information | 02203/40 22 22
  Road conditions | 11 69
  Weather forecast | 11 64
  News | 11 65

Allgemeiner Deutscher Automobil-Club (ADAC) | 3 79 90

Airlines
  Lufthansa | 82 68
  Lufthansa (at airport) | 02203/40 24 04
  British Airways | 13 50 81
  British Airways (at airport) | 02203/40 22 29

Lost property
  General | 1 77 11
  Cologne trams and buses | 54 71
  Federal Railways | 14 11

Taxis | 28 82

Telephone
  Services | 1 14
  Directory enquiries, inland | 1 18
  Directory enquiries, international | 0 01 18
  Exchange (inland) | 0 10
  Exchange (international) | 00 10
  Dialling code, United Kingdom | 00 44
  Dialling code, United States or Canada | 00 1

Preface

This Pocket Guide to Cologne is one of the new generation of Baedeker guides.

Baedeker pocket guides, illustrated throughout in colour, are designed to meet the needs of the modern traveller. They are quick and easy to consult, with the principal features of interest described in alphabetical order and practical details about location, opening times, etc., shown in the margin.

Each city guide is divided into three parts. The first part gives a general account of the city, its history, notable personalities and so on; in the second part its principal sights are described; and the third part contains a variety of practical information designed to help visitors to find their way about and make the most of their stay.

The Baedeker pocket guides are noted for their concentration on essentials and their convenience of use. They contain numerous specially drawn plans and coloured illustrations, and at the back of the book is a large plan of the city. Each entry in the main part of the guide gives the coordinates of the square on the plan in which the particular feature can be located. Users of this guide, therefore, will have no difficulty in finding what they want to see.

Facts and Figures

General

Cologne (in German Köln), a city and independent administrative district within the region of the same name and the *Land* of North Rhine – Westphalia, lies in latitude 50°56'33" N and longitude 6°57'32" E on both banks of the Rhine, within the Cologne Lowland (Kölner Bucht), an area bounded by the Bergisches Land and the hills of the Ville range. The old town centre lies on the left bank of the Rhine. The highest point within the city area is in the Königsforst (Royal Forest) to the SE of the city centre (116 m/382 ft); the lowest point is in the Worringer Bruch to the north (37·5 m/123 ft).

From within the Federal Republic: 0221
From the United Kingdom: 010 49 221
From the United States or Canada: 011 49 221

Telephone dialling codes

Cologne has an area of 405 sq. km/156 sq. miles, with 230 sq. km/89 sq. miles on the left bank of the Rhine. Its greatest length from east to west is 27·6 km/17·1 miles, from south to north 28·1 km/17·5 miles. It has a population of 1,016,000. Of the total area 174 sq. km/67 sq. miles are accounted for by arable land and gardens, grassland and forest; the rest is built up. The city's area represents 414 sq. m, or just under 500 sq. yds, per inhabitant.

Area and population

Cologne is divided into nine wards or districts (*bezirke*) with elected councils. The first ward (Innenstadt or Central Area) includes, on the left bank, the quarters known as Old Town South and North and New Town South and North (within the semicircle formed by Innere Kanalstrasse and Universitätsstrasse) and on the right bank the district of Deutz.
The other wards are:
2 – Rodenkirchen
3 – Lindenthal
4 – Ehrenfeld
5 – Nippes
6 – Chorweiler
7 – Porz
8 – Kalk
9 – Mülheim

City wards

The city's constitution, drafted on the British model in 1946, distinguishes between the city council, which takes decisions, and the administration, which carries them out. The chairman of the council is the elected Senior Burgomaster (Oberbürgermeister; the administration is headed by a chief official, the Oberstadtdirektor, who is assisted by 13 officers responsible for particular departments. The Council consists of 91 elected councillors. The Senior Burgomaster is assisted by three other burgomasters.

Administration

◄ *In the foreground, Great St Martin's Church; to the rear, the towers of the Cathedral*

9

Population and Religion

Population

The Roman settlement of Cologne, which was granted municipal status in A.D. 50, had a population of some 40,000. In later centuries the number of inhabitants showed a decline, but towards the end of the first millennium, with the town's development into an archiepiscopal see and an economic centre, the population began to increase again. During the medieval period Cologne seems to have had a population of at least 40,000. In 1794, at the beginning of the French occupation, the figure was 44,512.
The industrial age brought an explosive increase:
1821 –   55,355
1852 – 101,091
1890 – 281,681
1910 – 516,527
At the outbreak of the Second World War in 1939 the city had 768,352 inhabitants, but by the end of the war the population had shrunk to no more than 40,000. 81% of all dwellings in Cologne had suffered a greater or lesser degree of destruction, and in the city centre more than 90% of all houses had been totally destroyed. By 1946, however, the population had risen again to 491,380.

Religion

Christianised at an early stage (first Christian communities recorded in the 2nd c. A.D.) and from the 8th c. the seat of an archbishop with great influence in the Empire, Cologne remained a Christian city after the expulsion of the archbishops in 1288. Its great number of churches earned it the style, from the Middle Ages onwards, of "holy Cologne". During the religious conflicts of the Reformation the city remained Catholic, and it was not until 1802, during the French period, that Protestants and adherents of other creeds were permitted to live within the city area. After 1802 the influx of prosperous Protestant merchants gave a powerful impetus to Cologne's economic development. At the present time 62·7% of the city's German population is Roman Catholic and 28·3% Protestant.

Transport

Cologne's central situation at the intersection of important trade routes, and above all its location on the easily navigable Rhine, played a decisive part in the development of transport and traffic movement. During the Middle Ages the city had the farthest-flung trading network of all German towns.

Shipping on the Rhine

Cologne was particularly favoured by the circumstance that all goods transported on the Rhine had to be transferred here from vessels of greater draught to ships of shallower draught. Apart from the economic profit which the people of Cologne were able to draw from this (see Commerce and Industry), it led also to the construction of extensive port installations.
Cologne now has five harbour basins, with an annual turnover of over 13 million tonnes. In addition there is heavy passenger traffic (2·6 million passengers annually).

Road traffic

From time immemorial Cologne has been one of the great traffic intersection points of western Europe and in consequence one of the most important Rhine crossings. There are now eight bridges within the city area, including two rail and two motorway bridges. The motorway ring round the city links ten motorways, and in addition Cologne is served by twelve federal highways (Bundesstrassen) going in all directions. The movement of traffic into the city is facilitated by the urban motorway.

From the 1830s onwards Cologne developed into the fulcrum of rail traffic in western Germany. With the completion in 1859 of the first permanent bridge over the Rhine since Roman times, the important rail link between the two banks of the Rhine was opened up. In our own day the Central Station of Cologne is the busiest centre of passenger traffic in the Federal Republic, with some 1000 trains carrying anything up to 100,000 passengers a day.

Rail services

The Cologne-Bonn Airport, to the south-east of Cologne, is a modern and functional airport, conveniently linked with the city by motorway. In recent years, however, it has increasingly tended to be overshadowed by the nearby airports of Frankfurt (the Rhine-Main Airport) and Düsseldorf.

Airport

Culture

Cologne possesses the following municipal institutions: four theatres, seven museums, an art gallery, four archives, an

General

The main University building

orchestra, four libraries and 32 municipal branch libraries, nine higher educational establishments, the People's High School (an adult education centre) and the Rhineland College of Music. In addition there are numerous other institutions run either by private individuals or public bodies, ranging from a cabaret to a Roman Catholic social agency.

Higher educational
establishments

Cologne was the first town in Germany to have a municipal university (founded 1388), which was abolished in 1798 during the French occupation. The city had no college of commerce until 1899, when it was financed by Gustav von Mevissen and housed in neo-Baroque buildings in Claudius-strasse. The year 1919 saw the re-foundation, on the initiative of Senior Burgomaster Konrad Adenauer, of the University, which in 1928 moved into its new buildings, in functionalist style, in Universitätsstrasse, bordering the city's Inner Green Belt.

Since then the University has grown considerably in size and now has more than 50,000 matriculated students. In addition there are the Sports College (2500 students), the Technical College (8000 students), the Academy of Music, the Rhine-land College of Music, the Public Administration College and the Catholic College.

Libraries and archives

There are the University and City Library (1,663,000 volumes), the Central Medical Library (500,000 volumes), the Education Library, the Art Library of the Wallraf-Richartz Museum and 32 municipal libraries with a stock of some 923,000 volumes. There are a total of 15 archives, including those of the municipality. Among them are the Historical Archives (60,000 documents) and the Photographic Archives (more than 300,000 negatives).

Academies and learned
institutions

A leading place is taken by the Melanchthon Academy. Many learned institutions are associated with the University or with museums.

The following foreign cultural institutes are located in Cologne: Amerika-Haus, Belgisches Haus, British Council and French, Italian, Japanese and German-Finnish institutes.

Theatres and orchestras

In addition to the four municipal theatres (Opera House, Schauspielhaus, Kammerspiele and Puppet Theatre) and the municipal Gürzenich Orchestra, a major contribution to the city's cultural life is made by the West German Radio Corporation (Westdeutscher Rundfunk, WDR) with its various musical and dramatic presentations. There are also numerous non-municipal theatres and orchestras.

Commerce and Industry

General

Largely owing to its excellent situation at the meeting-place of trade routes Cologne achieved international status as a centre of commerce and industry from a very early period. The need to tranship here all goods transported on the Rhine led to the establishment of large markets, and merchants came to settle in the town. Staple Regulations of 1255 laid down that all vessels must display and offer for sale in Cologne, for three days, the goods they carried. As a result Cologne's trade during the Middle Ages became the most varied and far-flung in Germany; and the town's economic strength was a major factor in its early achievement of political independence. Cologne enjoyed a further growth of prosperity from the 19th c. onwards, based mainly on agriculture, mining and engineering.

Cologne's principal industries now are lignite mining in the Ville hills to the west of the city (and associated with this the generation of electricity), petrochemicals and refineries to the north and south, engineering (Klöckner-Humboldt-Deutz; the first four-stroke engine, the Otto engine, was constructed in Cologne about 1865), the Felten und Guilleaume cable factory, pharmaceuticals (Natterman & Madaus) and auto-mobile construction (Ford). Industrial establishments with over 20 employees have a total annual turnover of more than 25 billion DM.

Industrial and commercial activities

Cologne is also the principal shopping centre for an extensive surrounding area.

Since medieval times Cologne has been one of Germany's principal centres for banking of all kinds. Significantly, the first joint stock bank in Germany was established in Cologne in 1848; and the city still has an above-average number of private bankers.

Banking and insurance

Cologne's banks, and also its numerous insurance corporations, are concentrated in the city centre, particularly in and around Unter Sachsenhausen and Gereonstrasse.

Trade fair exhibition halls

Notable Personalities

Trade fairs

Trade fairs have a long tradition in Cologne, going back to the Staple Regulations of 1255 (which were merely a formal confirmation of older practices).

Cologne is now one of the world's leading trade fair centres, with 25 international fairs in its regular annual calendar (21,000 exhibitors from 90 countries, more than a million visitors annually), in addition to numerous other exhibitions and some 750 congresses and similar events every year. The city's trade fair organisation, an independent body known as Kölnmesse, has an annual turnover of some 110 million DM.

Tourism

Cologne has 238 hotels and other forms of accommodation with a total of over 10,000 beds and an annual figure of some 1·5 million "bed nights".

At times of particular pressure during trade fairs additional accommodation is provided in comfortable hotel ships on the Rhine.

Notable Personalities

Konrad Adenauer
German statesman
(1876–1967)

Adenauer, who had trained as a lawyer, was Senior Burgomaster of Cologne from 1917 to 1933. The city owes him a great deal – the reopening of the University in 1919, the laying out of the Green Belts with their recreational and sports facilities, the establishment of the Cologne Trade Fair in 1924 and the economic upsurge of the twenties. Dismissed by the Nazis in 1933, Adenauer lived in retirement during the Third Reich. After 1945 he again engaged in politics and became a co-founder of the conservative Christian Democratic Union (CDU); in 1948 he played a major part in the creation of the Basic Law of the Federal Republic of Germany, and in 1949 he became the first Federal Chancellor. During his period of office as Chancellor he left his mark on Germany's postwar history to an extent unequalled by any statesman of the day. He achieved the integration of the Federal Republic in the West (bringing the country, for example, into NATO) but at the same time re-established diplomatic relations with the Soviet Union and secured the repatriation of many prisoners of war. He gave up the Chancellorship in 1963.

Marcus Vipsanius Agrippa
Roman statesman and
general (64/63–12 B.C.)

Marcus Vipsanius Agrippa, a friend of the Emperor Augustus and his son-in-law (having married his daughter Julia), achieved fame both as a general and as a statesman. In 38 B.C., as governor of Gaul, he resettled a Germanic tribe, the Ubii, in the Oppidum Ubiorum, later to become Cologne. In 31, as commander of Augustus's fleet at the battle of Actium, he defeated the fleet of Antony and Cleopatra. He was also responsible for the construction in Rome of the Pantheon, as well as aqueducts and public baths, and for the preparation of a much admired map of the Roman Empire. His daughter Agrippina the Elder gave birth in Cologne in A.D. 15 to Agrippina the Younger (see entry), who secured for Cologne the status of a Roman *colonia*.

Konrad Adenauer

Julia Agrippina the Younger

Cardinal Josef Frings

Julia Agrippina was born in Cologne (then known as Oppidum Ubiorum), the grand-daughter of the town's founder Marcus Vipsanius Agrippa (see entry). Her brother was Caligula, Emperor from 37 to 41. Her first marriage, in 28, led to the birth of the future Emperor Nero. In 48 she married her uncle Claudius, Emperor from 41 to 54, and in 50 persuaded him to grant her the style of Augusta and to raise her native town of Cologne to the status of a *colonia*. Henceforth the town was known as Colonia Claudia Ara Agrippinensium (CCAA) and had an altar of the imperial cult. This was the origin of the city's present name.

In 54 Agrippina poisoned her husband Claudius in order to bring her son Nero, who was under her political influence, to the throne. In 59 Nero in turn caused his mother to be murdered.

Albertus Magnus (Albert the Great), who is believed to have been Count von Bollstädt, entered the Dominican order while studying in Padua. After teaching in various German monastic schools he took his degree as master of theology in Paris in 1247. In 1248 he was sent to Cologne to establish and direct a *studium generale* in the Dominican order there. His most celebrated pupil in Cologne was Thomas Aquinas (see entry). Albert's commentaries on Aristotle were important pioneering works. In addition to his theological studies he pursued scientific interests on a scale unusual in his day. His reputation was such that he was several times asked to act as arbiter in disputes between the burghers of Cologne and Archbishop Konrad von Hochstaden.

The remains of Albertus Magnus now rest in a sarcophagus in the crypt of St Andrew's Church.

Anno, scion of a knightly family of Swabia, began his career as chaplain to the Emperor Henry III, who appointed him Archbishop of Cologne in 1058. Never popular in Cologne, Anno was more interested in great matters of state than in his archiepiscopal duties. In 1062 he seized the person of the young Emperor Henry IV at Kaiserswerth in an attempt to win influence on the policies of the Emperor; but in this he had little

Julia Agrippina the Younger
(A.D. 15–59)

Albertus Magnus
German scientist,
philosopher and theologian
(c. 1200–1280)

Anno II (St Anno),
Archbishop of Cologne
(c. 1010–1075)

Notable Personalities

success, and was soon driven out. In 1074 he was compelled to flee from Cologne during a rising by the city's merchants, but was later able to suppress the revolt. He was responsible for the foundation or enlargement of many churches and religious houses, including Siegburg Monastery, where he was buried. In spite of the resistance he had aroused Anno was canonised in 1183.

Sulpiz Boisserée
German art scholar and collector (1783–1851)

Sulpiz Boisserée, born in Cologne, devoted himself from an early age, together with his brother Melchior, to the study of art, literature and philosophy. In Paris the brothers made the acquaintance of the great Romantic writer Friedrich Schlegel, who aroused their interest in Gothic architecture and in 1804 accompanied them back to Cologne. There they began to collect early German and Dutch paintings, many of them becoming available through the secularisation of church property. Their valuable collection was acquired in 1827 by King Ludwig I of Bavaria, and their pictures can now be seen in the Alte Pinakothek in Munich. – In 1808 Sulpiz began to produce drawings of Cologne Cathedral, with imaginative representations of the completed cathedral, and this promoted interest in the completion of the unfinished building. In 1835 he became provincial Curator of Artistic Monuments.

Heinrich Böll
German writer (1917–1985)

Heinrich Böll, a native of Cologne, began his career as a bookseller, but after the Second World War returned to the city, took up the study of German language and literature and soon afterwards became a professional writer.
Böll is one of the leading representatives of postwar German literature which has come to terms with the country's past. Among his best known novels are "Haus ohne Hüter" ("The Unguarded House", 1954), "Billard um halb zehn" ("Billiards at Half Past Nine", 1959), "Ansichten eines Clowns" ("The Clown", 1963) and "Gruppenbild mit Dame" ("Group Portrait with Lady", 1971). His book "Unter Kranenbäumen", with photographs by the celebrated photographer Chargesheimer, captures the atmosphere of the Cologne working-class district of Eigelstein. In 1972 Böll was awarded the Nobel Prize for literature, and in 1983, although attracting criticism for his strong political and social commitment, he was made an honorary citizen of Cologne.

Max Bruch
German composer (1838–1920)

Max Bruch was born in the Richmodis House in Cologne's Neumarkt. At first a conductor, he later turned to composition. His best known work is his violin concerto in G minor.

Bruno I (St Bruno)
Archbishop of Cologne (c. 925–985)

Bruno, the youngest brother of the Emperor Otto the Great, became Arch-Chancellor in 951 and Archbishop of Cologne in 953. Since he was also Duke of Lorraine, Cologne became the capital of his domains. He promoted monastic reform and learning. He is buried in St Pantaleon's Church, which he had had built.

Cardinal Josef Frings
German Catholic theologian (1887–1978)

Ordained as a priest in 1910, Josef Frings took his doctorate of theology in Rome in 1913, and in 1942 was appointed Archbishop of Cologne. He became a cardinal in 1946. He played an important part as chairman of the Fulda Conference of Bishops (1945–65) and at the Second Vatican Council. He was much loved by the people of Cologne for his sympathy and understanding during their years of hardship immediately after the Second World War. He retired from his post on age grounds in 1969.

Nikolaus Gülich, son of a well-to-do Cologne family, was responsible for the setting up in 1680 of a committee of investigation to enquire into bribery and corruption in the municipal council, and in 1683, with the help of the craft guilds, succeeded in having the whole council dismissed from office. The deposed councillors, however, appealed to the Emperor Leopold in Vienna and in 1685 secured the outlawing of Gülich and his friends. In the following year he was executed.

Nikolaus Gülich
(1644–86)

At first associated with Max Ernst and the Cologne Dada movement, Heinrich Hoerle founded in 1924 the Cologne "Group of Progressives", whose other members were Seiwert (see entry), Arntz, Freundlich, Adler and the photographer Sander (see entry). Hoerle, a Marxist, and Seiwert were perhaps the best of the group. Originally influenced by Expressionism and Cubism, Hoerle's style later owed much to the Russian Constructivists and Fernand Léger. His aim was to depict ordinary people and their lives in transparent (in the Marxist sense) reality. The declared aim of the group was to create "a new school of Cologne painters on a proletarian gold ground" – in a deliberate allusion to the great Cologne painting school of the Middle Ages. – Condemned as degenerate during the Nazi period, Hoerle died young of tuberculosis of the larynx. There are some of his pictures in the Ludwig Museum (Wallraf-Richartz Museum).

Heinrich Hoerle
German painter
(1895–1936)

Appointed Archbishop of Cologne in 1238, Konrad von Hochstaden was actively involved in regional political affairs, asserting and establishing Cologne's predominance in the lower Rhineland over the duchies of Jülich, Limburg, Brabant and Sayn, and was no less active in imperial politics, leading the opposition to the Emperor Frederick II and supporting rival claimants to the throne (Raspe, William of Holland, Richard of Cornwall).
In 1248 Konrad von Hochstaden laid the foundation stone of Cologne Cathedral. He was constantly in conflict with the burghers of Cologne, now becoming increasingly strong; in 1252 Albertus Magnus (see entry), called in as an arbiter, decided in favour of the burghers, and in 1255 Konrad granted the city the right of staple (trading and market rights), a major factor in its economic development. In 1257 he was defeated in the battle of Frechen, and in the following year Albertus Magnus again confirmed the burghers' rights. – Konrad's tomb is in one of the choir chapels in Cologne Cathedral.

Konrad von Hochstaden,
Archbishop of Cologne
(c. 1198–1261)

Leibl, born in Cologne, was originally apprenticed to a locksmith and later studied painting at the Munich Academy. He developed his own form of realism, which was highly praised by the celebrated French painter Gustave Courbet. After spending two years in Paris he returned in 1870 to Munich, where he became the leading figure in a group which also included Trübner, Schuch, Alt, Haider and Thoma. In 1873 he left Munich to live in the country, and thereafter devoted himself to depicting, with great fidelity of detail, the life of country people. His later pictures show some Impressionist features. The Wallraf-Richartz Museum has a number of his paintings.

Wilhelm Leibl
German painter
(1844–1900)

Notable Personalities

Stephan Lochner
German painter
(c. 1400–1451)

Stephan Lochner, the greatest master in the Cologne school of painters, whose work can be dated from 1430 onwards, created an unmistakable personal style, combining the strict idealising religious tradition of medieval painting with the "modern" realism of the Dutch school. In addition to such magnificent purely religious pictures as the "Madonna in the Rose-Garden" (Wallraf-Richartz Museum) and the "Madonna with Violet" (Diocesan Museum) Lochner – twice, in 1447 and 1451, a member of Cologne municipal council – painted the famous "Altar of the City's Patron Saints" (originally in the chapel of the town hall, now in the Cathedral), which gives expression to the confidence and independence of Cologne in a manner unique in the German painting of the period. – Stephan Lochner is believed to have died of plague in 1451.

August Sander
German photographer
(1876–1964)

August Sander, a native of Herdorf, began life as a miner, but in 1899 began to study photography in Trier. In 1910 he established a studio in Cologne, and from 1924 was a member of the "Group of Progressives" together with Hoerle and Seiwert (see entries). In 1929 he published his "Antlitz der Zeit" ("Face of our Time"), a magnificent depiction of people and their work in the twenties. His work fell into disfavour during the Nazi period, but after 1945 its qualities were again appreciated. His photographs of prewar Cologne (a number of which were acquired by the Municipal Museum in 1953) are not only of high artistic quality but are also a unique record of the city in earlier days. In 1962 Sander was awarded the Federal Cross of Merit (Bundesverdienstkreuz).

Franz Wilhelm Seiwert
German painter
(1894–1933)

Franz Wilhelm Seiwert, who, with Heinrich Hoerle (see entry), founded the "Group of Progressives" in Cologne in 1924, was the principal theorist of the group. His pictures, in a style which shows Cubist and Expressionist features, seek to depict the non-accidental element in reality, the situation of men and women in their social and professional setting. The Ludwig Museum (Wallraf-Richartz Museum) has some good examples of his work.

Friedrich Spee von
Langenfeld
German theologian and poet
(1591–1635)

Friedrich Spee von Langenfeld – priest, teacher and poet ("Trutznachtigall", mystical poems, 1649) – was one of the most vigorous opponents of the 17th c. persecution of alleged witches. In 1631 he published anonymously his "Cautio Criminalis", a fierce attack on the methods of trial practised in the witch-hunts. He died in Trier while caring for plague victims.

Thomas Aquinas
Scholastic theologian and
philosopher
(1225/26–1274)

Born in Aquino, near Naples, Thomas entered the Dominican order in 1243, and became a pupil in Cologne of Albertus Magnus (see entry), who exerted a powerful influence on some of his most fundamental ideas. From 1252 to 1259 Thomas lived in Paris, and later went to Rome. In 1272 he became director of the new *studium generale* established by the Dominicans in Naples.
Thomas Aquinas is recognised as the greatest philosopher and theologian of the Middle Ages. His acknowledgment of the legitimacy of learning alongside faith, while admitting the primacy of faith, is reminiscent of the teachings of his master Albertus Magnus. Thomas's ideas were also much influenced by Aristotle, whom he regarded as the philosopher *par*

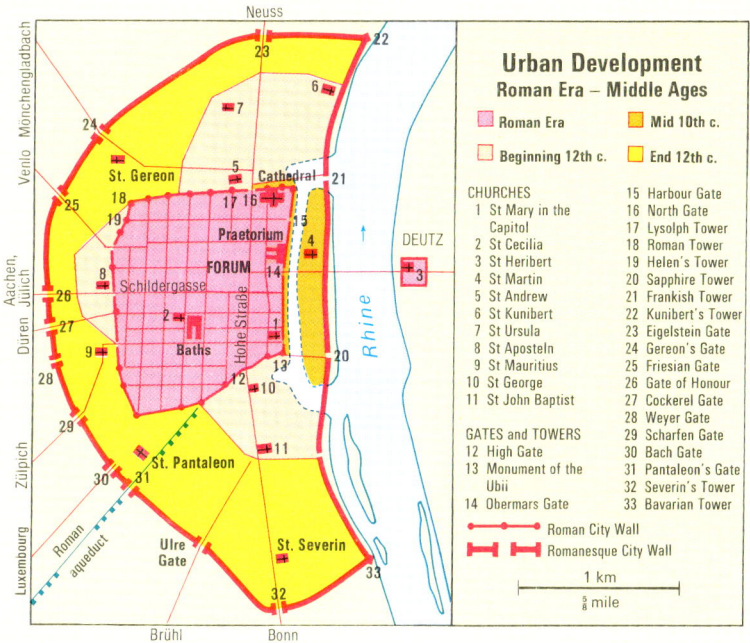

Urban Development
Roman Era – Middle Ages

| ■ Roman Era | ■ Mid 10th c. |
| □ Beginning 12th c. | ■ End 12th c. |

CHURCHES
1 St Mary in the Capitol
2 St Cecilia
3 St Heribert
4 St Martin
5 St Andrew
6 St Kunibert
7 St Ursula
8 St Aposteln
9 St Mauritius
10 St George
11 St John Baptist

GATES and TOWERS
12 High Gate
13 Monument of the Ubii
14 Obermars Gate

15 Harbour Gate
16 North Gate
17 Lysolph Tower
18 Roman Tower
19 Helen's Tower
20 Sapphire Tower
21 Frankish Tower
22 Kunibert's Tower
23 Eigelstein Gate
24 Gereon's Gate
25 Friesian Gate
26 Gate of Honour
27 Cockerel Gate
28 Weyer Gate
29 Scharfen Gate
30 Bach Gate
31 Pantaleon's Gate
32 Severin's Tower
33 Bavarian Tower

●━━━● Roman City Wall
■━■ ■━■ Romanesque City Wall

1 km
⅝ mile

excellence. His principal works are the "Summa Theologica" (1265–73), the "Summa contra Gentiles" (1261–64) and the "Quaestiones Disputatae" (1256–73). Thomas Aquinas was canonised in 1322 and declared a Doctor of the Church in 1567.

These two typical Cologne characters feature in countless local jokes and stories. Tünnes (the Cologne dialect form of Tony) is a short stout little man with a bulbous nose: good-natured, naive, but not entirely a fool. Schäl is tall and thin and has a squint; he is a sly and sometimes malicious character, who likes to pull people's legs and takes nothing seriously. The two are complementary to one another, representing as they do conflicting aspects of the Cologne character. There is a monument to them in the Martinsviertel (Rheinvorstadt).

Tünnes and Schäl
Cologne characters
(legendary)

19

History of Cologne

100,000 B.C.	Earliest evidence of occupation in Palaeolithic period.
From 5th c.	Bandkeramik (Ribbon Ware) settlements.
From 4th c.	Germanic settlements.
38 B.C.	The Ubii, a Germanic tribe, are resettled here by the Romans; construction of a fortified settlement.
A.D. 50	Julia Agrippina persuades her husband, the Emperor Claudius, to grant her native town, Cologne, the status of a *colonia*.
About 90	Cologne becomes capital of Lower Germany.
257–259	The Emperor Gallienus resides in Cologne.
310	The Emperor Constantine orders the construction of the first fortified bridge over the Rhine and the establishment of a fort at Deutz.
313	Maternus recorded as first bishop of Cologne.
355	The town is taken by Germanic tribesmen.
Before 450	Franks in Cologne.
6th c.	St Gereon's Church becomes the burial-place of Frankish kings.
About 665	First record of St Peter as dedication of the Cathedral.
About 785	Hildebold becomes archbishop of Cologne.
881	The town is stormed by the Normans, with severe destruction.
10th c.	First extension of the city, taking in the Rheinvorstadt (traders and merchants).
1028	The archbishop of Cologne is granted the exclusive right to crown the German king.
1031	The archbishop gains the dignity of Chancellor of Italy.
1074	First recorded dispute between the archbishop (Anno II) and the burghers of Cologne.
1106	The Emperor Henry IV grants the burghers of Cologne the right to fortify their town; second extension of Cologne.
1149	Earliest known use of the municipal seal; first reference to a Burghers' House, the predecessor of the Town Hall.
1164	Archbishop Rainald von Dassel brings the remains of the Three Kings (the Magi) to Cologne: a move calculated to strengthen the position of the Emperor Frederick Barbarossa in relation to the Pope.

Barbarossa confirms the burghers' right to build the highest and strongest town walls in Europe against the wishes of the archbishop.	1180
The foundation stone of the Cathedral is laid.	1248
Cologne is granted the right of staple (the right to trade and hold markets).	1255
Albertus Magnus mediates between the burghers and the archbishop.	1258
After winning the battle of Worringen the city gains its independence from the archbishop.	1288
Outbreak of plague and persecution of Jews.	1348
Work begins on the building of the Town Hall.	1359
A rising by the weavers' guild against the patrician rulers of Cologne is defeated.	1370/71
Foundation of Cologne University.	1388
The guilds are victorious over the patricians. Charter laying down the city's constitution.	1396
Expulsion of the Jews.	1424
Ulrich Zell establishes Cologne's first printing press.	1450
Cologne is officially recognised as a free city of the Empire.	1475
A rising against the municipal council is successful in securing an alteration of the city's constitution.	1512
Martin Luther's writings are publicly burned.	1520
Foundation of the Cologne Stock Exchange.	1553
Deutz is taken by Swedish forces; Cologne remains unscathed by the Thirty Years War.	1632
Nikolaus Gülich secures an investigation of corruption among members of the municipal council.	1680
Execution of Nikolaus Gülich.	1686
Cologne's first newspapers.	1734
The city is taken by French troops.	1794
The French close the University and abolish the holding of property by the church and by monasteries.	1798
Secularisation: members of non-Catholic denominations are allowed to settle in Cologne. Foundation of the Chamber of Commerce (the oldest in Germany).	1802
End of French rule.	1814

History of Cologne

1815	Cologne becomes Prussian.
1821	Re-establishment of the archbishopric of Cologne.
1842	Work is resumed on the Cathedral.
1859	Construction of the first permanent bridge over the Rhine in Germany since Roman times.
1880	Completion of the Cathedral.
1881	Cologne expands beyond the 1180 town walls, which are now pulled down.
1901	Foundation of the College of Commerce.
1914	Werkbund (Craft Union) Exhibition.
1919	Re-foundation of the University; demolition of the Prussian fortifications.
1924	Establishment of Cologne Trade Fair.
1925	Millennial Exhibition.
1938	In the "Crystal Night" the Cologne synagogues are set on fire.
1945	The city, almost completely destroyed, is taken by American troops.
1950	Celebration of Cologne's 1900 years of existence.
1959	Completion of the Severinsbrücke (St Severinus's Bridge).
1980	Centenary of the completion of the Cathedral; Pope John Paul II visits the city.
1983	The Rhine overflows, inundating the old town.

Sights from A to Z

**Altenberg Abbey

Altenberg Abbey, beautifully situated in the Dhünn valley, in the Bergisches Land (the area between the rivers Ruhr and Sieg), is one of the finest examples of Cistercian Gothic architecture in Germany.

It takes its name from the ancestral seat of the Counts of Berg, known as Altenberge, which was presented to the Cistercians by Count Adolf III, who then moved to his property of Neuenberge, near the present Burg Castle on the river Wupper. The monks began to clear the surrounding forests in 1183. The present Gothic church was built between 1259 and 1379, replacing an earlier Romanesque church. The church and the monastic buildings were badly damaged in 1815, when a dye factory installed in the former dorter during the period of French occupation was destroyed by fire. Rebuilding began in 1836.

Distance
30 km/19 miles NE

Bus
434 (from Breslauer Platz bus station)

Conducted tours
By appointment on weekdays
(tel. 02174/4282 or 4533)

Cathedral

In accordance with the severe rules of the Cistercian order the church is a plain building which draws its beauty from its clear proportions and the functional quality of its Gothic architecture. The absence of decoration reveals the structural principles of Gothic architecture in absolute purity: so far as possible the walls are dissolved into windows, and the weight of the stone masses is diverted into the regular structure of the buttresses. There is no tower: merely a modest roof turret crowning the church.

Exterior

In the interior the architecture serves as a frame, with restrained accents of red and green, for the famous stained glass windows, which, in accordance with Gothic conceptions, admit the light of the celestial Jerusalem. Particularly impressive, on account of their great size, are the west window (8 × 18 m/26 × 59 ft) with its gold-tinted glass (c. 1400) and the north window (6 × 19 m/20 × 62 ft), which is predominantly grey, with little colour (before 1300). The pure architectural forms are still more strikingly enhanced in the choir by the leaf patterns of the late 13th c. windows, which, in accordance with an old rule of the Cistercian order, are in tones of grey.

Interior

In front of the beautiful choir screen are, on right, a figure of St Bernard of Clairvaux and, on left, a figure of Moses (17th c.). Inset into the wall of the south aisle (windowless because of the cloister which formerly backed on to it) are a number of gravestones, the first of which (Abbot Johann Blanckenberg, d. 1662) is particularly fine. Also in the aisle are three wooden figures (17th c.) of SS. Cecilia, Mary and Barbara.

At the near end of the choir is a 16th c. Virgin in glory (modern). In the south transept is the modern organ. In the first arcade of the ambulatory can be seen the tomb of Prince Adolf VIII of Berg (14th c.), and farther east, set into the pavement, the

Furnishings

gravestones of one Gozelinus (12th c.). The Altar of the Virgin in the south choir aisle has figures belonging to a Coronation of the Virgin (15th c.). At the east end of the choir is a 15th c. altar cross, and just to the north of this a beautiful Late Gothic tabernacle (1490). In the choir chapels are the gravestones of various abbots, and a reliquary in the end chapel contains the heart of Archbishop Engelbert von Berg, murdered in 1225. On the east wall of the north choir aisle is the magnificent Annunciation (c. 1380) which was originally on the west doorway. In the choir arcades are two further monuments, the double tomb of Gerhard II (d. 1359) and his wife Margarethe and, farther west, the tomb of Archbishop Bruno III (d. 1200). The north transept is known as the Ducal Choir, after the eight tombs of Dukes of Berg which it contains. The first tomb (coming from the crossing) is that of the founder of the abbey, Adolf I. Above the tombs hangs the flag of Berg, and on the columns are hatchments. Farther west, on a pier, is a 16th c. wood figure of St Christopher.

Altenberg Cathedral is celebrated for its music; recitals are given every Sunday (except on special occasions) from May to October at 11.15 a.m. and 2.30 p.m. Information and programmes can be obtained from Stiftung Altenberg, Postfach 1165, Odenthal 1. At certain times there are also recitals on Thursday evenings at 8 p.m. of an international organ cycle.

Other buildings

The original entrance to the abbey ran to the west of the church, over the Dhünn on a bridge and through an 18th c. Baroque gateway (still preserved). In the central niche of the gateway arch are (outside) a figure of St Bernard of Clairvaux, second founder of the Cistercian order and preacher of the Second Crusade, and (inside) the Virgin.

By the bridge, on the left, is the Altenberger Hof, built on the foundations of the old porter's lodge and pilgrim hospice. To the right of the gateway there was a Lady Chapel, the remains of which are built into Haus Altenberg, erected in 1715.

The main conventual buildings lay to the south, with ranges of buildings running from north to south, separated by courtyards; only the lay brothers' range survives.

The most regrettable loss is the Late Romanesque cloister on the south side of the church, with stained glass depicting the life of St Bernard and the life of the Virgin (some of it preserved in the Schnütgen Museum (see entry) in Cologne).

St Mark's Chapel

To the north were various offices and the infirmary, of which there survives only St Mark's Chapel (1222; renovated 1899). Under the floor were found two other floor surfaces, the lower one giving evidence of the earliest building phase (12th c.).

The chapel is notable for its painted decoration, which dates from before 1300 (ornamental designs on central window behind the altar, Coronation of the Virgin on west wall); the windows date from about 1900. The chapel is still used for worship.

Altenberg Cathedral from the east ▶

The nave . . .   *. . . and the crossing*

Fairytale Forest

To the north of the abbey (10 minutes' walk) lies the Fairytale Forest (Märchenwald), with a series of little houses containing scenic representations of some of the best loved of Grimms' fairytales. By pressing a button, or in some cases by calling out, visitors can start a recording of the tale or set the figures in motion. The Fairytale Forest is open all day throughout the year. The restaurant is closed on Fridays.

Antonite Church (Antoniterkirche)

See Hohe Strasse and Schildergasse

Appellhofplatz   M9 (L24)

U-Bahn
Appellhofplatz

Trams
3, 4, 5, 9, 11, 12, 16

This square takes its name from the Prussian Court of Appeal, the highest court in the Rhineland province, which was established here in 1819. The semicircular layout of the court building was the work of Johann Peter Weyer (1826). It gave place between 1883 and 1893 to the present neo-Renaissance building, much simplified after the last war.
The atmosphere of the square has been somewhat spoiled by the modern headquarters of the West German Radio Corporation (WDR) on the south side.

*Arsenal (Zeughaus) and Municipal Museum M9 (L24)

The brick-built Arsenal was erected between 1594 and 1606. The rear front, on the street known as An der Burgmauer, rests on the foundations of the Roman town walls. At the east end is the Roman Fountain (Römerbrunnen), constructed in 1915 in the form of the foundations of one of the Roman towers on the walls. On the fountain are twelve heads, carved in relief, of the Roman Emperors from Augustus to Theodosius. Above them is a quotation from Tacitus's "Annals" referring to Cologne.
The entrance to the Arsenal and the Municipal Museum is in Zeughausstrasse. (The difference in level between Zeughausstrasse and the street to the rear, An der Burgmauer, demonstrates how the Romans took advantage of the configuration of the land in laying out the town walls). The Renaissance entrance doorway is crowned by the city's coat of arms, topped by a helmet and surrounded by allegorical figures. The staircase tower on the west wall follows the pattern of similar towers on old patrician houses in Cologne. Adjoining on the west is the Prussian Old Guardhouse (Alte Wache) of 1840–41.

The Municipal Museum is mainly devoted to items illustrating the history of Cologne since medieval times. Among objects of particular interest are the Romanesque (12th c.) and Gothic (13th c.) municipal seals, the charter of 1396 laying down the city's constitution and a very fine model of the medieval town. Other items of interest include furniture, arms and armour, flags, etc.

Location
Zeughausstrasse

U-Bahn
Appellhofplatz

Trams
3, 4, 5, 9, 11, 12, 16

Opening times
Tues.–Sun. 10 a.m.–5 p.m.;
Thurs. 10 a.m.–8 p.m. (when special exhibitions)

Municipal Museum

The Arsenal, which now houses the Municipal Museum

*Assumption, Church of the (St Mariä Himmelfahrt)   L9 (L25)

Location
Marzellenstrasse 32–40

U-Bahn
Dom/Hauptbahnhof

Buses
132, 133

Trams
5, 9, 11, 12, 16

Opening times
Throughout the day; nave
only during services

This former Jesuit church, one of Cologne's few Baroque churches, is rated one of the finest examples of Jesuit Baroque in Germany. The Jesuits, who are first recorded in Cologne in 1544, began the building of the church in 1618; the architect was Christoph Wamser. The construction was financed by munificent donations, particularly from the Wittelsbachs, who were Electors of Cologne in the 17th c. The church was finally consecrated in 1678. After suffering heavy destruction during the Second World War it was restored to its original form by rebuilding work which was completed in 1983.

The church gives expression to a specific programme. Just as the Jesuits saw themselves during the conflicts of the Reformation and the wars of religion as the champions of the old true faith, so their magnificent new church was designed to reflect the tradition of faith in the tradition of architecture. The large window in the west front, Baroque though that is, has Gothic tracery; and both the towers flanking the west end and the bell-tower at the east end (visible from the square outside the station) have Romanesque elements.

Interior

The combination of the styles of different periods can be seen also in the interior. The disposition of the windows, the decoration and the furnishings are in the spirit of the early Baroque period, but individual architectural features, such as the traceried windows, are quotations from earlier periods.

Furnishings

The furnishings (by Jeremias Geisselbrunn and Valentin Boltz) are also conceived with a doctrinal purpose, being directed towards the glorification of the Virgin (whose role was disputed by the Reformers), though reflecting at the same time a distinctive Cologne tradition. As in the high choir of the Cathedral, there are free-standing figures of the Virgin and Christ on the piers of the choir (east end) and of the twelve Apostles on the piers of the nave. The typically Jesuit attitude to the Virgin is given expression in the symbolic effigies of her in the arcading of the aisles. The high altar (1628), crowned by a Madonna in glory, has as its principal painting an Assumption of 1643.

Other features of interest are the pulpit (1634), the Lady Altar (1628) in the south choir aisle, a communion bench of 1724, paintings in the choir by Johann Toussyn and 17th c. confessionals in the aisles.

On the north side of the church is the former Jesuit College, now the offices of the vicar-general. On the south side are the ABC Building of 1976 – an unfortunate intrusion into the setting of the church – and a number of 18th and 19th c. burghers' houses.

Baroque splendour in Augustusburg Palace ▶

Augustusburg Palace (Schloss Augustusburg), **Brühl**

Distance
12 km/7½ miles S

Tram
KBE, route 18
(from Barbarossaplatz)

Opening times
Feb.–Nov., 9 a.m.–noon and
2–4 p.m. (except last
weekend in month)
Closed: Mon.

Augustusburg Palace, once residence of the archbishops of Cologne, a magnificent example of Baroque and Rococo architecture, is situated half way between Cologne and Bonn. A moated castle built in 1284 and soon afterwards enlarged served as one of the residences of the archbishops after they were driven out of Cologne in 1288. The castle was destroyed in 1689, and in 1725 the foundation stone of the present palace was laid by Clemens August of Wittelsbach (1700–61), bishop of Münster, Paderborn and Hildesheim, archbishop and elector of Cologne, Grand Master of the Teutonic Order and the possessor of many counties and duchies, who was a rather inept ruler but a great lover of the arts and of falconry. The original design was prepared by the Westphalian architect Konrad Schlaun, but his plans were considerably altered by François Cuvilliés, who took over the work in 1728.

In addition to the architect a number of other prominent artists were involved, including Balthasar Neumann (the staircase hall) and Carlo Carlone (ceiling paintings). The palace was completed in 1768.

During the French occupation from 1794 onwards almost all the furniture disappeared, and in 1944 the palace suffered severe damage, the north wing being worst affected. The palace now belongs to the *Land* of North Rhine-Westphalia and is used for the reception of high political personalities as guests of the *Land* government.

Exterior

The palace is approached from the east. From this side visitors can admire Schlaun's U-shaped plan, with the north and south wings flanking the grand courtyard. The east sides of the wings preserve Schlaun's original Baroque conception. Under Cuvilliés' direction the south side of the palace became the main front; but since this involved altering part of the structure which had already been built the south front is asymmetric.

Interior

The entrance to the palace (conducted tours only) is in the north wing, opening off the grand courtyard. Particularly notable is Balthasar Neumann's magnificent staircase hall, culminating in the ceiling fresco (a pyramid bearing the initials of Clemens August, surrounded by allegorical figures, personifications of the arts and of divinities, overthrowing the forces of evil), which splendidly displays the self-confidence of absolutist power.

On the upper floor of the west and south wings are an imposing succession of rooms, differing in design but all lavishly appointed. Although some of these rooms may be designated as bedrooms, etc., these too were originally used for receptions and ceremonial purposes.

On the lower floor are the Summer Apartments, also used for receptions, etc., but mainly in summer. They are given an affect of coolness by the use of blue and white wall tiles (from Rotterdam).

Gardens

The gardens on the south side of the palace were designed by Dominique Girard. With their regular layout of flowerbeds and pools they are a typical example of the French style of horticultural planning. The view from the south, looking over the central avenue, the Mirror Pool (with fountain) and the carefully designed gardens towards the palace, expresses the very spirit of 18th c. absolutism, deliberately setting out to control nature as it controlled the state.

The palace church (entrance in Schloss-strasse, at the NW corner of the rear front of the palace), originally a Franciscan church consecrated in 1493, was refashioned in Baroque style from 1735 onwards. The main feature of the simple interior is the high altar designed by Balthasar Neumann, in the centre of which is a revolving mirror with the symbol of the Trinity. The Prince Elector was accustomed to sit behind this and, by turning the mirror, watch the worshippers kneeling in front of the altar without himself being seen.

Church

1·5 km/1 mile SE of the palace (reached by a 20–30 minutes' walk through the park, or by car) is the hunting lodge of Falkenlust. Clemens August was a passionate falconer, seeing falconry not only as a sport but, symbolically, as an exercise of the keen perception and discipline required for the conduct of the state. The records show that in the year 1748 he spent some 10,000 thalers on hunting, two-thirds of it on falconry.
Falkenlust was built to provide a convenient base for hunting parties, but also for secret negotiations and gallant adventures. Designed in Rococo style by Cuvilliés and Leveilly, it was begun in 1729. The decoration, both externally and internally, incorporates hunting themes. Notable features are the Lacquer Cabinet (with a painted portrait of Clemens August), the tiled staircase hall and, on the upper floor, the Mirror Room.

Falkenlust

Balchem House (Haus Balchem)   N9 (O25)

Balchem House is Cologne's finest surviving Baroque mansion, built by a brewer named H. Deutz in 1676; the date is inscribed on the gable. Although the façade is Baroque it still shows the traditional structure of a medieval Cologne house (see Overstolz House): above the ground floor is a mezzanine floor with an oriel window, above this the main floor with living accommodation, and above this three floors of attics and store-rooms.
The house is now occupied by a branch of the People's High School (adult education centre), with a library.

Location
Severinstrasse 15

Buses
132, 133

Trams
6, 15, 16

*Bazaar de Cologne   M8 (M23)

This complex (designed by Gruhl and Gerling, 1980–81), built round a central courtyard, is an interesting attempt to solve a problem which crops up frequently in Cologne, the filling in of a gap site. This concrete and steel structure, lying between Mittelstrasse and Brinkgasse, is finished entirely in white, with much use of glass, and touches of green provided by plants and grass. The two-storey inner courtyard has a glass roof borne on white steel beams. The complex was deliberately designed to include dwellings and offices as well as shops. In spite of a rather trendy design (with shops to match) the Bazaar is a lively and cheerful place.

Location
Mittelstrasse

U-Bahn
Neumarkt

Buses
136, 146

Trams
1, 2, 3, 4, 7, 9, 11, 12, 16

Botanic Garden

See Flora Park and Botanic Garden

*Brauweiler Abbey

Buses
961, 962 (from Breslauer
Platz bus station, platform
3A)

Distance
13 km/8 miles W

Opening times
Usually closed on weekdays

Exterior

The village of Brauweiler, now incorporated in Pulheim, lies
west of Cologne in the beautiful country rising towards the Ville
hills. In these hills, near Brauweiler, are the extensive lignite
workings of the Rhine-Westphalia Electricity Company, which
has its largest transformer station here.
The abbey, dedicated to St Nicholas, was founded in 1024 by
Mathilde, wife of Count Palatine Ezzo and daughter of the
Emperor Otto II and Empress Theophano, on the site of earlier
buildings dating from the 6th c., and was occupied by
Benedictines from Trier. The present church shows a mingling
of different periods of Romanesque architecture, from about
1050 to the 13th c., with Gothic additions.

The church's towers are a prominent landmark, rising out of the
surrounding plain. The imposing west end (c. 1140) with its
helm-roofed tower (1515) is 69 m/226 ft high. The roof, over
the simple nave and the 13th c. choir in the High Romanesque
style of the Rhineland, is dominated by the octagonal tower
over the crossing with its flanking towers (13th and 19th c.).

Lady Altar, Brauweiler Abbey

The entrance to the church is at the NW corner of the Baroque conventual buildings (18th c.). The west doorway within the porch, with relief decoration, dates from the 12th c.

Interior

In the interior of the church the Romanesque forms of the walls in the nave, crossing and choir (raised because of the crypt beneath) and the Late Gothic vaulting of the nave with its painted foliage decoration combine in harmonious unity. There are interesting remains of medieval painting on the piers of the choir and nave.

Particularly notable items in the richly furnished interior are the Renaissance altar of St Anthony in the south transept, a beautiful Lady Altar of 1180 in the south choir aisle and the figure of the foundress (c. 1200) over the south door.

Furnishings

The choir screen has fine Romanesque relief work. At the east end of the choir is the communion bench, decorated with carving (1731). The choir-stalls date from 1700. At the east end of the choir is St Bernard's Chapel, over the entrance to which (columns with fine capitals) is a cross of about 1400. In the north choir aisle is an impressive seated figure of St Nicholas (12th c.); in the arch over the north doorway a figure of Count Palatine Ezzo; in the north transept a 16th c. altar of St Michael; and in the north aisle very fine confessionals of 1724.

The entrance to the crypt is beside the steps leading up to the crossing. The oldest parts of the crypt, which was altered about 1200 on the model of St Maria im Kapitol (see entry), date from about 1050.

Crypt

Other features of interest are the cloister on the south side of the church (entrance from south aisle), which dates from before 1200 (west and north sides destroyed about 1810); the chapterhouse on the east side of the cloister, with notable 12th c. ceiling paintings in the beautiful Romanesque vaulting (fine capitals); and the Lapidarium, with unique relief-decorated gravestones of the 11th c. (representations of Christ, the Apostles and the signs of the zodiac).

Bottmühle

See Romanesque town walls

Brühl

See Augustusburg Palace

Carthusian Church (Kartäuserkirche)   O9

Although the founder of the Carthusian order, St Bruno (d. 1101), came from Cologne, the Carthusians established themselves in the town only in 1334. The church, in Carthusian Gothic style, was consecrated in 1393; the Chapel of the Angels and Lady Chapel (with figural consoles of outstanding quality) were added on the north side of the church in the 15th c. The closed monastic accommodation, with 25 cells and

Location
Kartäusergasse 7–9

Buses
132, 133

Trams
6, 15, 16

33

a chapterhouse built round a cloister on the south side of the church, has not survived, but the 18th c. conventual buildings to the west of the church have been restored for use as the Church House. The church itself is now the Protestant parish church.

The line of the walls in Kartäusergasse and Ulrichgasse still marks the corner of an area of 5 morgens (just over 3 acres) of arable land which was presented to the Carthusians in 1337 by a Cologne patrician named Konstantin von Lyskirchen.

**Cathedral (Dom) M9 (L25)

U-Bahn
Dom/Hauptbahnhof

Buses
132, 133

Trams
5, 9, 11, 12, 16

Opening times
Throughout the day
Treasury 9 a.m.–5 p.m., Sun.
12.30–5 p.m.

Conducted tours
11 a.m., 2.30 p.m., 3.30 p.m.

Organ recitals
June-Aug., Tue. at 8 p.m.

Designed by its builders to be the largest cathedral in the world, Cologne Cathedral (dedicated to SS. Peter and Mary) is still one of the largest buildings in Christendom. Cologne's great landmark and emblem, it represents the culmination and final fulfilment of Gothic cathedral architecture.

The impulse for the building of the cathedral was politically motivated. In 1164 Archbishop Rainald von Dassel, the Emperor Frederick Barbarossa's chancellor, caused the remains of the Three Kings (the Magi) to be brought to Cologne; and in the Middle Ages the Three Kings were regarded as the prototypes and symbols of kingship, so that possession of their relics was seen as legitimising royal authority – an authority which Barbarossa was concerned to assert in his conflict with Pope Alexander III to secure papal recognition. The relics were originally housed in the old cathedral built (818 onwards) by Archbishop Hildebold, Charlemagne's counsellor, on the site of earlier structures which had themselves been erected in the 4th and later centuries on the foundations of Roman temples. In 1248 Archbishop Konrad von Hochstaden laid the foundation-stone of the present cathedral, which was to be built, not in the Romanesque style which had produced so many notable churches in Cologne but on the model of the French royal cathedrals in the new Gothic style. The resting-place of the Three Kings was to stand out royally among the other churches of Cologne.

The first architect of the cathedral, Gerhard, drew on the full range of contemporary architectural knowledge and skills in the designing of his building. The sacristy (now the Chapel of the Sacrament) was completed in 1277, the choir in 1322. Thereafter building made slow progress, largely because of the immense cost, which was met by donations and the sale of indulgences. By 1560, when building came to a halt, the whole area of the planned cathedral had been at least temporarily roofed and the choir had been closed off with a wall at the west end; but the 58 m/190 ft high stump of the south tower with its crane was to remain for centuries a feature of the landscape in Cologne.

Building was resumed in 1842, following the revival of interest in the Middle Ages during the Romantic period of the early 19th c., and the national enthusiasm which saw the completion of the cathedral as a symbol of German unification, as well as the discovery in 1814 of the original 13th century plan of the west front. The foundation stone was laid by King Frederick William IV of Prussia, and the completion of the building in

The Cathedral, Cologne's principal landmark ▶

Buttresses

Vaulting of the choir

1880 was marked by a ceremony at which the German Emperor William I was present – though Archbishop Melchers was not, in consequence of the conflict between church and state in Prussia. – It can be said, however, that the cathedral has never actually been completed. The authorities responsible for its maintenance are constantly engaged in restoration work, not only to make good war damage but also, above all, because the polluted air of the industrial age is continually eating away the stone.

It is estimated that between 1824 and 1961 some 40 million DM were spent on the cathedral. Part of the cost was met by the Cathedral Building Lottery (which still exists); the rest came from local cathedral taxes, donations from the Cathedral Building Association and state subsidies. The cost of the first building phase, up to 1560, cannot be estimated.

Exterior

The men of the 13th c. saw the Gothic cathedral as a likeness of heaven, with its towers and turrets standing for the City of God. Accordingly it was relieved of all feeling of weight, all the various parts of the building were dematerialised and the walls became no more than a framework for the great areas of window. In the 7000 sq. m/8400 sq. yds of the west front there are no walls to be seen: the towers rear up to their height of 157 m /515 ft in a pattern of windows, buttresses and tracery. On the west front is the cathedral's oldest doorway, St Peter's Door (to the south). Some of the fine robed figures in the style of the Parler family of sculptors can be seen in the Diocesan Museum (see entry).

Cathedral
of St Peter and St Mary

Cathedral Church of the
Archbishopric of Cologne

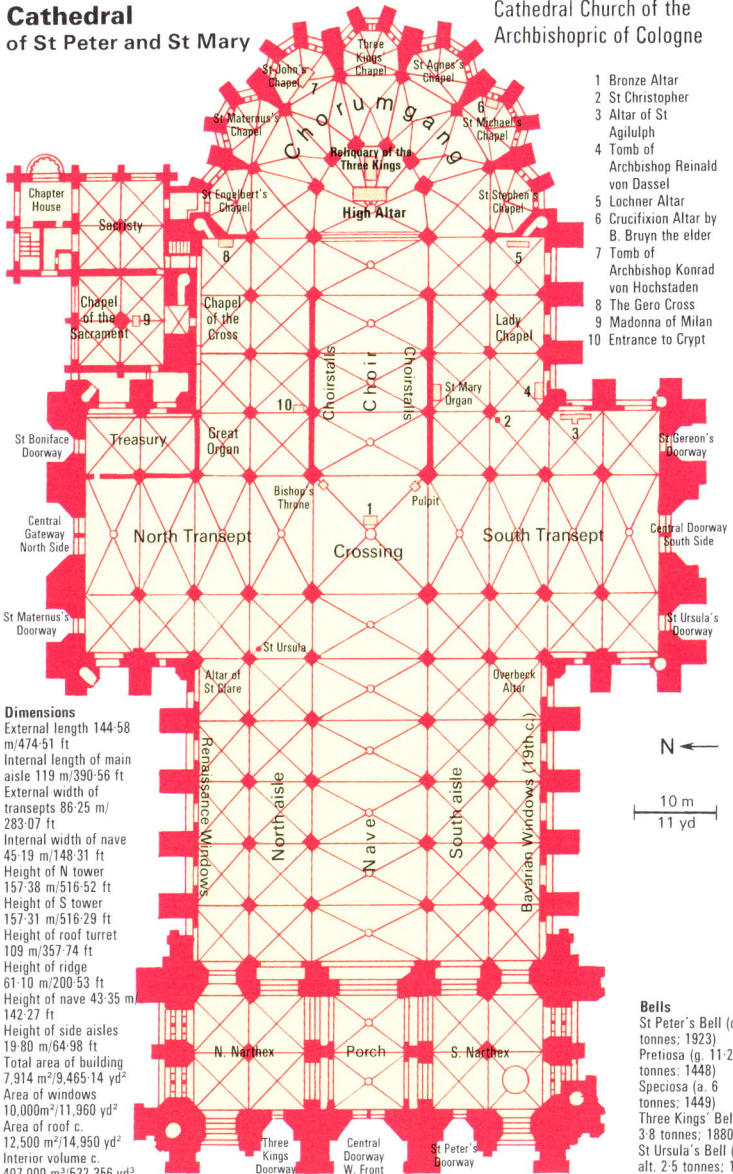

1 Bronze Altar
2 St Christopher
3 Altar of St
   Agilulph
4 Tomb of
   Archbishop Reinald
   von Dassel
5 Lochner Altar
6 Crucifixion Altar by
   B. Bruyn the elder
7 Tomb of
   Archbishop Konrad
   von Hochstaden
8 The Gero Cross
9 Madonna of Milan
10 Entrance to Crypt

Three Kings' Chapel
St John's Chapel
St Agnes's Chapel
St Maternus's Chapel
St Michael's Chapel
Chorumgang
Reliquary of the Three Kings
St Engelbert's Chapel
St Stephen's Chapel
High Altar
Chapter House
Sacristy
8
Chapel of the Sacrament
9
Chapel of the Cross
5
Lady Chapel
St Mary Organ
Choir
10
Choirstalls
Choirstalls
4
2
St Boniface Doorway
Treasury
Great Organ
St Gereon's Doorway
Central Gateway North Side
Bishop's Throne
1
Pulpit
Central Doorway South Side
North Transept
Crossing
South Transept
St Maternus's Doorway
St Ursula's Doorway
St Ursula
Altar of St Clare
Overbeck Altar

N ←

10 m
11 yd

Dimensions
External length 144·58
m/474·51 ft
Internal length of main
aisle 119 m/390·56 ft
External width of
transepts 86·25 m/
283·07 ft
Internal width of nave
45·19 m/148·31 ft
Height of N tower
157·38 m/516·52 ft
Height of S tower
157·31 m/516·29 ft
Height of roof turret
109 m/357·74 ft
Height of ridge
61·10 m/200·53 ft
Height of nave 43·35 m/
142·27 ft
Height of side aisles
19·80 m/64·98 ft
Total area of building
7,914 m²/9,465·14 yd²
Area of windows
10,000m²/11,960 yd²
Area of roof c.
12,500 m²/14,950 yd²
Interior volume c.
407,000 m³/532,356 yd³

Renaissance Windows
North aisle
Nave
South aisle
Bavarian Windows (19th c.)

N. Narthex
Porch
S. Narthex

Three Kings' Doorway
Central Doorway W. Front
St Peter's Doorway

Bells
St Peter's Bell (c. 24
tonnes; 1923)
Pretiosa (g. 11·2
tonnes; 1448)
Speciosa (a. 6
tonnes; 1449)
Three Kings' Bell (b.
3·8 tonnes; 1880)
St Ursula's Bell (c. in
alt. 2·5 tonnes; 1862)

Cathedral

The "framework" pattern of Gothic architecture can be seen even more clearly in the side walls of the cathedral, with its forest of piers and buttresses taking up the thrust of the stone masses and creating an effect of weightlessness. The end of the south transept (with fine bronze doors by Ewald Mataré, one of them depicting Cologne in flames during the Second World War) dates from the 19th c.; the choir is 13th c. The end of the north transept suffered heavy damage during the war, and restoration was completed only in 1982.

Interior

The spirit of Gothic architecture is again revealed in the interior. This mystical space, the boundaries of which are difficult to distinguish through the dissolution of the walls into windows, receives its light from the vividly coloured windows – light which seems to come from some supra-terrestrial world. The vaulting is borne on more than a hundred piers. This image of the celestial city is a work of perfect harmony: all its dimensions are fractions or multiples of the lateral measurements of the crossing (14·45 m/47·4 in.), so that, for example, the height and width of the nave are three times this figure, the average distance between the piers half the figure.

The keystone of the crossing weighs over 9 tonnes. In 1852 a schoolmaster named Caspar Garthe suspended a 40 m/130 ft pendulum from it in order to demonstrate the rotation of the earth.

Furnishings

The windows in the south aisle were presented by King Ludwig I of Bavaria in 1842. It is planned to set up the so-called Overbeck Altar, with an "Assumption" (19th c.), at the east end of the aisle.

On the east side of the south transept is the altar of St Agilolphus (from Antwerp, 1521), with a "Deposition" and a "Lamentation" in the centre. On a pier near the crossing is a figure of St Christopher, 3·70 m/12 ft high, by Tilman van der Burch (1470).

Chapels

The most celebrated painting in the Cathedral, Stephan Lochner's Altar of the City's Patron Saints (Altar der Stadtpatrone), erroneously referred to as the Dombild (1445), has been housed since 1956 in the first choir chapel. Originally in the chapel of the Town Hall (see entry), this painting symbolised the pride and self-confidence of the burghers of Cologne, who are represented in the picture as having direct access to the Virgin through the city's patron saints, SS. Gereon and Ursula and the Three Kings, without the mediation of any ecclesiastical or secular lord. – At the west end of the chapel is the tomb of Archbishop Rainald von Dassel.

In the next chapel, to the left, is a magnificent window with Biblical scenes (1280), from the demolished Dominican church.

The central window in the next chapel is also from the Dominican church. The altar (1548) was the work of Barthel Bruyn the Elder. The end chapel (next but one), which formerly housed the reliquary of the Three Kings, also has very fine stained glass. The central window is the oldest in the cathedral (1260), with Old Testament scenes on the left prefiguring the New Testament scenes on the right. The other two windows date from 1320.

The Lochner altar

Reliquary of the Three Kings

Cathedral

High choir and Reliquary of
the Three Kings

The religious and political programme of the cathedral finds its
clearest expression in the high choir (which can be entered
only on conducted visits).

At the east end of the choir is the Reliquary of the Three Kings,
one of the great masterpieces of medieval goldsmith's work,
created in 1181 and following years by Nicholas of Verdun and
his pupils. The finest parts are the lower sections of the sides,
with figures of prophets and kings which were the work of
Nicholas himself. On the front, which is of pure gold (presented
by King Otto II in order to secure the support of the influential
city of Cologne in the affairs of the Empire), are representations
of the Adoration of the Kings (with Otto behind them, to
the left, as the fourth monarch) and the Baptism of Christ,
with Christ enthroned above. On the rear of the reliquary, in
the middle register, is a portrait of Archbishop Rainald von
Dassel.

The high altar is one of the largest in Christendom
($4 \cdot 52 \times 2 \cdot 12$ m/$14 \cdot 8 \times 7$ ft). On the front are fine 14th c. figures.
The choir-stalls (1310), magnificently carved with both
religious and secular scenes, were occupied by the cathedral
chapter and provost, with stalls also for the Emperor and the
Pope – a total of 51 persons. Above these terrestrial personages
there unfolded a programme of decoration which moved
steadily away from the terrestrial to the celestial. First there
were the legends painted on the altar rails (14th c.): for example
the story of Pope Silvester and the Emperor Constantine
acknowledging each other's legitimate rights – expressing not
so much the historical reality as a piece of wishful thinking.
Then follow, on the piers, the Apostles, Christ and the Virgin, as
pillars of the church (noble 13th c. work). Finally there is the
"sea of glass" of the Book of Revelation in the windows
(13th c.): along the sides the 24 kings of Judah and the 24
elders of the Apocalypse, at the east end the Three Kings
(making altogether 51 kings to match the number of choir-
stalls) – reflecting the glory of the courts of heaven on the
terrestrial scene below. The chapel immediately to the north of
the most easterly chapel contains the tomb of Archbishop
Konrad von Hochstaden (13th c.). The classical beauty of the
recumbent figure has led this work to be compared with Greek
sculpture. The windows are 13th and 14th c.

On the east wall of the Chapel of the Cross (Kreuzkapelle: the
last chapel before the transept) hangs the Gero Cross, the
oldest in the cathedral. The cross, which follows Byzantine
models, was commissioned by Archbishop Gero (10th c.), who
secured the Byzantine princess Theophano as the Emperor
Otto II's bride. – A doorway in the north wall of the chapel leads
into the Chapel of the Sacrament (Sakramentskapelle), with
the famous Milan Madonna of about 1280.

Crypt

The crypt (entrance below the organ) contains archbishops'
tombs and the foundations of Archbishop Hildebold's earlier
cathedral.

Treasury

The Treasury (entrance at the NE corner of the north transept)
contains a remarkable collection of liturgical objects and
utensils. A sensation was caused in 1975 when thieves broke
into the Treasury and stole a number of valuable works of art;
one of the most important items, the Golden Monstrance of
1657, was melted down by the thieves for easier disposal (a
replica is being prepared). In addition to reliquaries, shrines and

Figures of Apostles

monstrances, items of particular interest in the Treasury include a number of illustrated medieval manuscripts, in particular the Hillinus Codex (1025) from the island of Reichenau, with a dedicatory picture showing Archbishop Hildebold's cathedral. Among other treasures is a monstrance of 1500 with links of a chain, said to be the chain with which the Apostle Paul was bound.

On a pier at the east end of the north aisle can be seen a 16th c. figure of St Ursula with protective cloak. Nearby is the fine altar of St Clare (Clarenaltar), with paintings of 1350 and 1400 (restoration completed 1982), which came from a convent of Poor Clares, now destroyed. The windows in the south aisle are 16th c.; in the second and fourth from the east, at the foot, are the figures of donors, surrounded by their family coats of arms. (Each member of the chapter was required to show that he had 16 ancestors of noble blood, here represented by the coats of arms).

Aisles

The south tower of the cathedral can be climbed (509 steps; open 9 a.m.–5 p.m., in winter until an hour before the onset of darkness). The stairs lead up to the bell chamber; the most notable bells are those known as Peter (1923, 24 tonnes), Pretiosa (1448, 11·2 tonnes) and Speciosa (1449, 6 tonnes). Beyond this the ascent (partly on a spiral staircase) continues to an outlook platform (fine views) at 97·25 m/319 ft.

South tower

41

Central Station (Hauptbahnhof) **L/M9 (L25)**

U-Bahn
Dom/Hauptbahnhof

Buses
132, 133

Trams
5, 9, 11, 12, 16

Cologne's first railway station was built in 1857 on a site previously occupied by the Botanic Garden. Of the new station built in 1890–94 there survives only the large platform hall (255 m/837 ft long, 65 m/213 ft wide, 24 m/79 ft high), bearing witness to the technological optimism of the period. The form of the steel construction shows some similarities with the Gothic architecture of the Cathedral (see entry) a short distance away.

The entrance hall was built in 1951–57. The station restaurant (now with a self-service counter), on a lower level, reflects the Art Nouveau style of 1910.

Conception, Church of the (St Mariä Empfängnis)

See Minorite Church

Corpus Christi Church

See Ursuline Church

*Diocesan Museum (Diözesanmuseum) **M9 (L25)**

Location
Roncalliplatz 2

U-Bahn
Dom/Hauptbahnhof

Buses
132, 133

Trams
5, 9, 11, 12, 16

Opening times
Weekdays (except Thurs)
10 a.m.–5 p.m.,
Sun. 10 a.m.–1 p.m.

This little museum in the shadow of the Cathedral (see entry) has a fine collection of art, mainly religious, from the Frankish period onwards. Founded in 1858, it moved into its present quarters in 1972.

The following items are of particular interest:

In the entrance hall are a number of figures, of high artistic merit, from St Peter's Doorway and the south tower of the Cathedral. Some of them were the work of the Parler family of sculptors, who created what is known as the "beautiful style" in the second half of the 14th c.: in the centre of the room five Apostles (c. 1380), on the walls angels and prophets (c. 1340), together with gargoyles and pinnacles.

In the room over the staircase, in two cases to the left, are two important assemblages of grave goods from a woman's and a boy's grave of the Frankish period, found in a burial chapel under the Cathedral. These tombs, evidently belonging to members of princely families, give evidence of the importance of Cologne in Frankish times, a period about which little is known from other sources.

In another case, to the right, is the interesting Severinus Disc, all that remains of an 11th c. reliquary of St Severinus. Bishop Severinus (whose existence is attested in the 4th c.) is shown with the incorrect title "archiepiscopus" (archbishop).

Beyond this is the famous "Madonna with Violet" (c. 1440) by Stephan Lochner, the leading member of the Cologne school of painters (see Notable Personalities).

Note also the very fine Romanesque capitals (c. 1200).

Dionysus Mosaic

See Roman-Germanic Museum

Eigelstein Gate (Eigelsteintor)

See Romanesque town walls

Eigelstein quarter — L9 (K25)

This part of Cologne, like the Severinsviertel (see entry), grew up along the axis of the Roman road to Neuss and around the convents of St Ursula and St Cunibert (see entries). Flanking the road were Roman cemeteries, the discovery of which during the Middle Ages gave rise to a flourishing cult of (and trade in) relics.

The modern development of the district began in the 1860s to house the growing population of Cologne in the industrial age. Many old house-fronts in the late neo-classical style of the period have survived.

A central feature of the Eigelstein quarter is the fortified Eigelstein Gate (Eigelsteinstorburg) in the Romanesque town walls (see entry), which during the urban development of the 1880s determined the line of the Neusser Strasse and later the siting of St Agnes's Church (see entry).

Destruction during the last war and the piercing of new traffic arteries (through route from north to south) have destroyed a large part of the Eigelstein quarter, but it still preserves much of its old character and atmosphere – an atmosphere into which incomers settle very comfortably. The considerable problems of slum clearance and rehabilitation are being carefully and skilfully tackled.

U-Bahn
Ebertplatz

Bus
148

Trams
5, 6, 9, 10, 11, 12, 15, 16

*El-De-Haus — M9 (L24)

This house, built by a Cologne businessman named Leopold Dahmen in 1934–35, was taken over by the Gestapo in 1935 and converted for use as their headquarters, with offices on the upper floors and a prison and torture chambers in the basement. The building was restored in 1980–81 and opened to the public as a memorial. Evidence of the sufferings of the people who were murdered here – often being crowded more than 30 to a cell with an area of no more than 9 sq. m/100 sq. ft – is provided by over 1200 inscriptions on the walls; some of them are in Cyrillic script, since the prisoners included Russians.

Nothing is left of the places of torture and execution. There is a small room containing very informative documentary material.

Location
Appellhofplatz 23–25

U-Bahn
Appellhofplatz

Trams
3, 4, 5, 9, 11, 12, 16

Opening times
Tues.–Sun. 10 a.m.–5 p.m.

Falkenlust

See Augustusburg Palace, Brühl

Flora Park and Botanic Garden   J/K10

Location
Am Botanischen Garten

Buses
134, 148

Trams
11, 15, 16

Cologne's first Botanic Garden gave place in the mid 19th c. to the Central Station (see entry); then in 1862 the present Flora Park, designed by Peter Joseph Lenné on the initiative of a number of wealthy citizens of Cologne, took its place. To this English-style park the Botanic Garden was added in 1914.

Of the original buildings only the Palm House (1863) survived the last war; it is now used as a restaurant. The gardens are much frequented both for recreation and for botanical studies.

4711 House   M9 (M24)

Location
Glockengasse

U-Bahn
Neumarkt

Trams
1, 2, 3, 4, 7, 9, 11, 12, 16

The name of the famous 4711 eau de cologne (Kölnisch Wasser) dates from the period of French occupation around 1800, when all the buildings in Cologne were numbered and this house was given the number 4711. After the Second World War the handsome neo-Gothic façade was re-erected with a new building behind. On the façade are a carillon and a clock with mechanical figures.

Gerling Corporation Offices (Gerling-Konzern)   M8 (L23)

Location
Gereonshof/Klapperhof

Trams
6, 10, 15

The offices of this large corporation (insurance, etc.) were built in the area to the west of St Gereon's Church (see entry) from 1930 onwards. Of particular interest are the Ehrenhof (Am Gereonshof), built by Arno Breker after the Second World War in the monumental style of the Third Reich, and the Rotunda (Im Klapperhof), designed by Breker, Müller and Sobottka. The neo-Gothic building (1893–97) formerly occupied by the Municipal Archives, with its handsome façade, was preserved by being incorporated in a new building.

*Great St Martin's Church (Gross St Martin)   M9/10 (M26)

Location
Martinspförtchen 8

Buses
132, 133

Trams
1, 2, 7

Standing out until the mid 19th c. as a major Cologne landmark near the unfinished tower of the Cathedral, the massive central tower of St Martin's still rises imposingly out of the maze of streets in the Martinsviertel (see Rheinvorstadt). The first buildings on the site were erected on the foundations of Roman warehouses associated with the old harbour on the Rhine; then in the 10th c. Archbishop Bruno founded a college of canons, later converted into a Benedictine house. The present church was consecrated in 1172 by Archbishop Philipp von Heinsburg. The tower over the crossing was built between 1185 and 1220. The present Gothic spire replaced the earlier Romanesque tower roof in the 15th c. The reconstruction of the exterior after war damage is now practically complete.

The façade on the Rhine consists of a trilobate choir similar to that of the Holy Apostles (see entry). The heavy structural masses are skilfully broken up by the rich articulation of the

Offices of the Gerling Corporation

Choir of Great St Martin's

walls, particularly on the square tower with its four corner turrets. The horizontally articulated Romanesque forms are extended vertically upwards, already prefiguring the principles of Gothic architecture. The modelling of the nave is much plainer.

The interior is impressive particularly for its height (25 m/82 ft). Here too, and particularly in the trilobate choir, the upwards movement of the forms can be seen. A trilobate choir has a trefoil ("clover") shape with three "leaves" called conches which are usually domed. The crossing is roofed with a dome. Since the restoration of the interior is not yet complete, the furnishings have not been replaced.

Green Belts (Grüngürtel)   K8–O8

The Versailles Treaty of 1919 called for the demolition of Cologne's fortifications, built during the Prussian period in replacement of the old Romanesque town walls (see entry). Credit for the laying out of the Inner and Outer Green Belts in their place is due to Senior Burgomaster Konrad Adenauer and the city architect, Fritz Schumacher. They were deliberately designed to provide facilities for recreation, with numerous ponds and sports grounds.

The Inner Green Belt, 7 km/4½ miles long, extends in a semicircle from the Gereon Goods Station in the north to Luxemburger Strasse in the south, bounded on the outside by Innere Kanalstrasse and Universitätsstrasse. In this ring, near the Aachener Weiher (pond), are the Museum of East Asian Art and the new University (see entries). The little hills in the green belt are built up from the rubble of buildings in the city centre destroyed by bombing.

The Outer Green Belt extends for 30 km/20 miles from Müngersdorf in the west to Rodenkirchen on the Rhine.

*Gürzenich and Old St Alban's Church   M9 (M25)
(Alt St Alban)

Location
Martinsstrasse 29–31

Buses
132, 133

Trams
1, 2, 7

The Gürzenich was built in 1437–44 to the design of the municipal architect Johann von Bueren as a public building serving a variety of purposes, such as was commonly found in the large and prosperous towns of the period. The ground floor was used as a warehouse and store, while on the upper floor there was a banqueting hall (23×53 m/75×174 ft) with an open timber roof. Several Emperors were entertained here (Frederick III in 1474, Maximilian I in 1486 and 1505, Charles V in 1520). Later the Gürzenich served only as a warehouse, until in the early 19th c. it recovered its function as a place for receptions and celebrations. It is now used for public events of various kinds.

Exterior of the Gürzenich

The Gothic architecture contains features of both civil and religious building, for example the battlements round the roof or the decorative elements. Between the windows are coats of arms. The main front is on the east side of the building; above the entrance are statues of Marcus Vipsanius Agrippa, founder

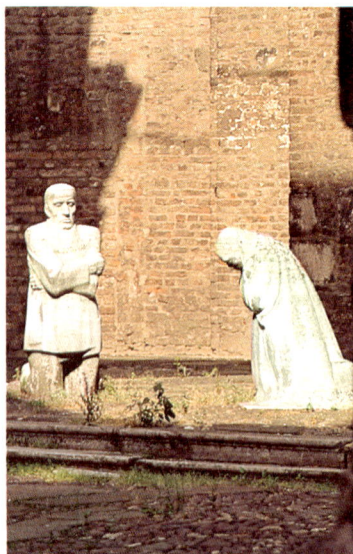

"Mourning Parents", Old St Alban's

Gürzenich Cultural Centre

of Cologne in the 1st c. B.C., and Marsilius, defender of the town during the Roman period.

The interior was destroyed during the last war and has not been restored in its original form. On the ground floor is a restaurant, while the upper floor is still used for receptions and other public occasions.

Interior of the Gürzenich

From the staircase of the Gürzenich and from the street called Quatermarkt it is possible to look into the ruins of Old St Alban's Church, which was destroyed during the last war and is now a memorial to the dead of the two world wars, with the "Mourning Parents" (copy of a work by Käthe Kollwitz, 1931).

Old St Alban's

Hahnentor

See Romanesque town walls

*Heinzelmännchen Fountain (Heinzelmännchenbrunnen)   M9 (L25)

The Heinzelmännchen Fountain (1899) has reliefs round the sides relating the story of the Heinzelmännchen, the industrious little men who appeared at night and secretly did the work of all the people who had been too idle to do it themselves. All would have gone well but for a tailor's wife who scattered peas about on the floor to take them by surprise; after which the little men disappeared and have never been seen again. The central section of the fountain shows the woman, with a lamp, and the little men tumbling down the stairs.

Location
Am Hof

U-Bahn
Dom/Hauptbahnhof

Buses
132, 133

Trams
5, 9, 11, 12, 16

Herz-Jesu-Kirche (Church of the Sacred Heart)   N8 (O23)

The Herz-Jesu-Kirche, built in 1893–1900, is one of Cologne's most important neo-Gothic buildings, clearly influenced by the Cathedral (see entry), which had been completed in 1880. The nave is for all practical purposes a postwar rebuilding; the original character of the church is best seen in the tower.

Location
Zülpicher Platz 16

Trams
6, 7, 10, 15

Heumarkt (Haymarket)

See Rheinvorstadt

Hohe Strasse and Schildergasse   M9 (L25, M24/25)
(Pedestrian zone)

The Hohe Strasse (High Street) follows the line of a prehistoric track running along the bank of the Rhine above flood level, which in Roman times formed the *cardo maximus* of the settlement, linking the north gate and the road to the military camp at Neuss with the south gate and the road to the camp at

U-Bahn
Dom/Hauptbahnhof

Buses
132, 133

The Hohe Strasse shopping centre

In the Antonite Church

Man of Sorrows (Church of the Holy Apostles)

Bonn. It has preserved its importance as a central axis of the city down to the present day, but it is now, together with Schildergasse (in medieval times the street of the shield-painters) which joins it at right angles, a pedestrian zone with numerous shops.

Trams
5, 9, 11, 12, 16

Boat landing-stages
1, 2, 3, 4, 7, 9, 11, 12, 16

At Schildergasse 57 stands the 14th c. Antonite Church (Antoniterkirche), a small aisled and vaulted basilica. In the north choir aisle is a memorial to those killed in the war, with Ernst Barlach's "Angel of Death" (second casting, 1938; the head has the features of the artist and sculptress Käthe Kollwitz).

Antonite Church

---

*Holy Apostles, Church of the (St Apostel)   M8 (M23)

The Church of the Holy Apostles is famous for its trilobate choir (see Great St Martin's Church), perhaps the most harmonious example of the type. The church as a whole, however, is a masterpiece of the Romanesque architecture of the Hohenstaufen period.
The first church on the site was erected in the 10th c. In the 11th c. Archbishop Pilgrim built a basilican church, apparently oriented to the west, just outside the Roman walls, which until the 12th c. formed the boundary of the monastery precinct. The west tower dates from the 12th c. The trilobate choir at the east end of the church was built after 1192 as a counterpart to the west choir. At the beginning of the 13th c. the basilican aisled nave was vaulted. Restoration work carried out since 1945 has brought the church back to its 13th c. form.

The main front of the church is the east end, looking on to the Neumarkt (formerly the cattle market). The three conches of the trilobate choir cluster round the octagonal drum of the dome over the crossing, which is topped by a small lantern. Sharp accents are added to the solid structure of the church by the two helm-roofed turrets set at the junctions of the three conches. The building is given a rich horizontal articulation by the two-storey structure of the choir with a dwarf gallery running round the top, a type characteristic of the Hohenstaufen period, on the model of the church at Schwarzheindorf, near Bonn, or St Gereon's (see entry). Seen from the Neumarkt the west tower fits into the background of the roof pattern, but from the west the very different fortress-like character of the west end is revealed. The rhomboid helm roof of the west tower appears to have been the prototype of this roof form in Hohenstaufen architecture.

Within the church the massive rectangular hall at the west end with its open tower (under the organ gallery lies the 11th–12th c. crypt, reopened in 1955) and the trilobate choir form a curiously harmonious composition. The success of the combination of two very different elements is due in large measure to the vaulting of the nave. The two-storey horizontal articulation of the walls, particularly in the choir, reflects the articulation of the exterior. In the choir itself, in contrast to St Mary's in the Capitol (see entry), the centralising effect is still further enhanced by the dome, the octagonal drum of which is carried on squinches over the piers of the crossing.

Location
Apostelnkloster 10

U-Bahn
Neumarkt

Buses
136, 146

Trams
1, 2, 3, 4, 7, 9, 11, 12, 16

Opening times
Closed at lunchtime; choir open only for services

Exterior

Interior

In the south-west transept, by the entrance, are statues of the 14 Auxiliary Saints (15th–17th c.). On the east wall is a 16th c. Lady Altar.

The modern altar and canopy (by S. Hürten, 1975) have been the subject of much controversy; they are believed by many to disturb the harmony of the trilobate choir.

On the south-east pier of the crossing is a Madonna of 1300.

A fine 14th c. series of Apostles, whose proper place is in the east choir, are at present in course of restoration.

On the north-east pier of the crossing is a 15th c. figure of St George.

In the north-west transept can be seen a very fine "Man of Sorrows" by Tilman van der Burch (15th c.).

Beside the stairs leading up to the organ are Baroque figures of SS. Peter and Paul.

Furnishings

---

*Knechtsteden Monastery

The history of this monastery, beautifully situated amid orchards, began in 1130, when the Dean of Cologne Cathedral, Hugo von Sponheim, presented the site to the Premonstratensian order. The construction of the choir and transept of the church was begun in 1138 by Provost Christian, and soon afterwards Dean Albertus Aquensis began the nave and the western apse. A goldsmith named Albert financed the building of the conventual buildings to the north of the church, and much restoration and new building has been carried out since the end of the 19th c. After the destruction of the eastern apse by the troops of Charles the Bold of Burgundy about 1475 it was rebuilt in Gothic style by Abbot Ludger. The monastery was dissolved during the period of French occupation. In 1869 it was damaged by fire. Restoration work started in 1878; the present state of the buildings is the result of further restoration carried out in 1962–64.

Distance
28 km/17 miles NW

Access
Train to Dormagen, then bus

There is an attractive view of the church from the east (approaching it through Baroque monastery gateway). The Gothic choir contrasts sharply with the mature Romanesque forms of the octagonal tower over the crossing (similar to the tower of St Andrew's Church in Cologne) and the two towers flanking the choir. The nave and western apse are impressive in their simplicity.

Exterior

The interior, with its pure Romanesque forms and the light-filled elegance of the Gothic east choir, is also very simply conceived. The wall paintings in the western apse (12th c.) are of more than regional importance. The central feature is the figure of Christ as Judge, enclosed within a mandorla, surrounded by the symbols of the four Evangelists and flanked by Peter and Paul. Round the windows are the other eleven Apostles. Kneeling at Christ's feet, on the left, is Albertus Aquensis. Unlike other surviving 12th c. paintings in the Cologne area (St Mary's in Lyskirchen (see entry)), the Knechtsteden paintings are clearly in the Byzantine tradition with its strict control of form.

Interior

◀ *Church of the Holy Apostles: the choir*

Knechtsteden Monastery

Christ in a mandorla

In the squinches of the dome over the crossing are some remains of Late Gothic painting. A 14th c. Pietà can be seen on the SW pier of the crossing. The new altar cross has a Christ of 1760.

Furnishings

Ludwig Museum

See Wallraf-Richartz Museum

Martinsviertel

See Rheinvorstadt

*Minorite Church (Minoritenkirche)

M9 (M25)

The church is dedicated to the Conception of the Virgin (St Mariä Empfängnis).

There is evidence of the presence of Minorites – the order of Friars Minor founded by St Francis of Assisi – in Cologne as early as 1229; but owing to the resistance of the established orders it was not until 1245 that they were able to begin the construction of their friary on the present site which was presented to them by the Bishop of Liège. The choir was consecrated in 1260, and the nave and cloister followed in the 14th c. The restoration of the severe damage suffered by the church during the last war was completed in 1958.

The plain Gothic architecture of the exterior, without transept or tower, reflects the ideal of the mendicant friars, and the interior of this aisled basilica shows the same simplicity, with only the scantiest ornament. Its great charm lies in the clarity of its lines. On the SW circular pier is a painted 14th c. Crucifixion, discovered in 1956.

On the south side of the choir, in the Chapel of the Sacrament, can be seen the tomb of Adolph Kolping (1813–65), founder in 1849 of the Cologne Gesellenverein, a Catholic organisation concerned with the welfare of young workers.

The dominating feature of the choir is a winged reredos of 1480 from Alfeld which was brought to Cologne after the Second World War. On the central panel is a standing figure of the Virgin as Queen of Heaven.

In the north aisle, outside the sacristy, is the Brauweiler Cross (1024), which was presented to Brauweiler Abbey by Mathilde, wife of Count Palatine Ezzo. The cross itself is the original one, but the figure of Christ is 14th c.

Also in the north aisle is a monument (1957) to the famous Scottish-born scholastic philosopher Johannes Duns Scotus, who in 1308 became a teacher at the monastic school here. Duns Scotus was one of the earliest theologians to concern himself with the problem of the Virgin's immaculate conception; and, appropriately, he is buried in this Church of the Conception.

To the north-west of the church is a statue of Adolph Kolping. Remains of the old cloister can be seen from the courtyard of the Wallraf-Richartz Museum (see entry).

Location
An Minoriten

U-Bahn
Appellhofplatz

Trams
3, 4, 5, 9, 11, 12, 16

Opening times
Throughout the day

Nave of the Minorite Church

The Alfeld Virgin

Müngersdorf Stadium (Müngersdorfer Stadion)   M/N3

Location
Aachener Strasse,
Müngersdorf

Tram
1

The Müngersdorf Stadium was built in 1923, at the same time as the Outer Green Belt (see entry) was laid out. The two brick-built wings which survive from the original structure were designed by Adolf Abel (1926). The new stadium, with covered seating for 60,000 spectators, was built in 1973–75. Around the stadium are a variety of sports facilities. A large tramway station was also provided to cope with the thousands of fans who come to big matches.

Municipal Gardens

See Stadtgarten

Municipal Museum

See Arsenal

Museum of Applied Art

See Overstolz House

54

*Museum of East Asian Art (Museum für Ostasiatische Kunst) N7

The core of this museum, the oldest European museum concerned solely with East Asian art, was a collection presented to the city in 1909 by Adolf and Frieda Fischer. Since then the collection has been increased by donations and purchases, and in addition it receives items on loan from the National Museum of Korea. The museum's original premises were destroyed during the Second World War, and it now occupies a remarkable new building by the Aachener Weiher (pond), designed by the Japanese architect Kunio Mayekawa, a pupil of Le Corbusier; it was opened in 1977. The architect has contrived to give a Far Eastern atmosphere to the building by such features as the reddish-brown tile cladding of the exterior, the Japanese garden (designed by Masayaki Nagare) in the inner courtyard and the subtly oriented relationship of the building and its terrace (restaurant) to the Aachener Weiher.
The collection comprises material from China, Korea and Japan ranging from the Bronze Age to modern times. Only a selection (periodically changed) can be shown at any given time; in addition there are regular special exhibitions on particular aspects of East Asian art and culture.

Location
Universitätsstrasse 100

Trams
1, 2

Opening times
Tues.–Sun. 10 a.m.–5 p.m.
1st Fri. in month
10 a.m.–8 p.m.

Conducted tours
Sun. at 11 a.m. and by arrangement (tel. 40 50 38); cultural films from East Asia, Tues. and Sat. at 3 p.m.

Museum of Ethnology (Museum für Völkerkunde)

See Rautenstrauch-Joest Museum

Neumarkt (New Market) M8/9 (M24)

This square, which has been in existence since the 11th c., was originally used as a livestock market; later, particularly during the Prussian period, it served as a drill ground. It is now a centre of the business world. A Christmas market is held in the square in December.

U-Bahn
Neumarkt

Trams
1, 2, 3, 4, 7, 9, 11, 12, 16

Of the old buildings which formerly flanked the square there remain only the Church of the Holy Apostles at the north-west corner and the Richmodis House, as rebuilt in 1928, on the north side. On the upper floor of the tower (modelled on the old towers of Cologne) of the Richmodis House are two horses' heads, alluding to the story of a Cologne woman called Richmodis von Aducht. The story goes that Richmodis, who had apparently died and had already been buried, suddenly appeared at the door of her house. Her husband refused to believe that she had returned from the dead, swearing that his horses would sooner run up the steps to the tower than his wife come back to life: whereupon he heard the clatter of hooves as his horses raced up the stairs.
The composer Max Bruch was born in the Richmodis House in 1838.

Richmodis House

At the south-east corner of the square stands Wolf Vostell's "Traffic at a Standstill" monument – a car concreted into place, usually covered with posters and placards, forming an ironic commentary on the traffic chaos in the square.

"Traffic at a Standstill" monument

Kunsthalle

Beyond this is the People's High School (Adult Education Centre), which conceals the Kunsthalle (Art Hall; periodic special exhibitions), which is also the headquarters of the Cologne Art Union, and the Central Library.

Neustadt

See Rings

New St Alban's Church (Neu St Alban) L8

Location
Gilbachstrasse 25

This notable modern church at the north-west corner of the Stadtgarten (see entry) was built by Hans Schilling in 1957–59 to replace Old St Alban's, the parish church of the old town, which was destroyed during the last war. Bricks from the old Opera House, also destroyed during the war, were used in its construction. Pentagonal in plan, with a high apse at the east end, it is modelled on Le Corbusier's chapel at Ronchamp in Lorraine.

Of particular interest is the layout of the interior, designed to accord with the new liturgical ideas then coming forward. The altar is so placed that the celebration of the mass takes place facing the congregation – a conception which became official only at the Second Vatican Council. On the north side is a Chapel of the Sacrament.

New St Alban's Church

Some of the furnishings from Old St Alban's (see entry) are now in the new church: a 16th c. Crucifixion at the west end, the Apostles on the organ gallery, the 15th c. Pietà below the organ and the beautiful Baroque pulpit.

New St Heribert's Church (Neu St Heribert)   M10 (M27)

This church, built at the end of the 19th c., is a characteristic example of the trend of that period in Cologne to return to the forms of 12th c. Romanesque architecture. Its main feature of interest, however, is the reliquary of St Heribert in the choir, brought here from Old St Heribert's (see entry). This is one of the finest pieces of goldsmith's work from the Rhine-Meuse area in the period 1160–70.

Also in the choir are a number of Baroque figures from Old St Heribert's.

Location
Deutzer Freiheit 64

Trams
1, 2, 7

Opening times
Throughout the day

Old Market (Alter Markt)

See Rheinvorstadt

Old St Alban's Church (Alt St Alban)

See Gürzenich and Old St Alban's Church

Old St Heribert's Church (Alt St Heribert)   M10 (M27)

Cologne's 3rd c. Roman fort (see entry) became a royal stronghold during the Frankish period; then in 1002 the Emperor Otto III presented the site to his friend Archbishop Heribert, Chancellor of the Empire, who founded a Benedictine abbey and built a church dedicated to the Virgin. The original church, which has not survived, was designed on a central plan and, according to the records of the time, was built by "foreign architects", probably from Byzantium. In the 10th–11th c. the Benedictine theologian Rupert of Deutz, author of an important commentary on Ezekiel, taught in the monastic school.

In consequence of its situation across the river from Cologne the abbey was frequently involved in conflict with the city and other external enemies (including particularly the Archbishop of Cologne), and was several times destroyed and rebuilt. The present Baroque church dates from the 17th c., the conventual buildings to the east from the 18th. Restored after war damage, the abbey is now an old people's home. Unfortunately the setting of the church and the abbey has been severely impaired by the Lufthansa building, a tower block erected in the 1970s. The church's greatest treasure, the reliquary of St Heribert, is now in New St Heribert's Church (see entry).

Location
Urbanstrasse

Trams
1, 2, 7

Opening times
At present closed

Opera House and Theatre (Opernhaus, Schauspielhaus)   M9 (M24)

Location
Offenbachplatz

U-Bahn
Neumarkt

Buses
136, 146

Trams
1, 2, 3, 4, 7, 9, 11, 12, 16

Cologne's new Opera House, built in 1954–57 to the design of Wilhelm Riphahn and H. Menne, replaces the old Opera in Rudolfsplatz which had been destroyed during the war. The building is functional, but has the presence worthy of an important public building, with the sloping sides of the rear portion giving it a distinctive character.

On the east side of the Opera House is the new Theatre, built in 1960–62.

A plaque on the Glockengasse side of the Opera House commemorates the synagogue on this site (by Ernst Friedrich Zwirner, 1859) which was destroyed in 1938.

Overstolz House (Museum of Applied Art)   N9 (N26)

Location
Rheingasse 8

Buses
132, 133

Trams
1, 2, 7

Opening times
Tues.–Sun. 10 a.m.–5 p.m.

Conducted tours
By arrangement
(tel. 2 21 38 60)

Museum of Applied Art
(Kunstgewerbemuseum)

Overstolz House (Overstolzenhaus), now occupied by the Museum of Applied Art, is the finest example in Germany of a burgher's house of the Romanesque period. It was built by the Overstolz family in 1220–30 in the Rheinvorstadt (see entry), long the preferred area for the residences of wealthy patrician families, particularly merchant families.

The Overstolzes played a major role in the conflict between the burghers of Cologne and Archbishop Engelbert von Falkenburg, taking part in the fighting and helping to defeat the archbishop's forces at the Ulre Gate (Romanesque town walls (see entry)).

The combination of living quarters and business premises in the same building is characteristic of the houses of wealthy merchants in the Middle Ages. This pattern is reflected on the gable front with its handsome round-headed windows.

On the ground floor were the entrances and various halls and lobbies; the original entrances were replaced in the 19th c. by the three round-arched windows to the right. The large rooms on the first floor, the *piano nobile*, were used for social occasions. Above this, within the gable, were four floors of warehouses and store-rooms. Right at the top can be seen the boom of a derrick used for hoisting goods up into store. It is evident, therefore, that the greater part of the building, including the cellars, was used for business purposes; and the effect of the whole structure was to proclaim the status of the well-to-do middle class of merchants.

As a result of alterations made over the centuries and destruction during the last war, the interior of the house has preserved little of its original character. After restoration it now houses the Museum of Applied Art.

The Museum of Applied Art was founded in 1888 on the initiative of a number of Cologne citizens. The collection comes partly from donations, partly from purchases financed by contributions from members of the Kunstgewerbeverein (Association of Arts and Crafts).

In consequences of the vicissitudes of its history and the loss of the original museum building of 1897 in the Second World War the museum's collections are now housed at a number of

Overstolz House ▶

different places in the city. Overstolz House has been its main centre, for display and for storage, since 1961.

The museum puts on regular exhibitions of material from its extensive collections, sometimes devoted to particular themes. The reserve collections can be seen only by appointment.

*Phantasialand (Recreation Park)

Location
Berggeiststrasse 31–41,
Brühl bei Köln (on B 51); by
rail to Brühl, then shuttle bus

Distance
15 km/9 miles S

Opening times
Daily, end Apr. to end Oct.

The Phantasialand Recreation Park, to the south of Cologne near Brühl (see Augustusburg Palace), offers a variety of entertainment and fun for all ages.

The attractions include a "dome cinema" (in which the films are projected on to the surface of a dome), a switchback, a water-chute, a Casa Magica, in which the law of gravity is apparently suspended (e.g. with water seeming to run uphill), a monorail, a dolphin show, a reproduction of old Berlin, a pirate ship, Chinatown (with a performance by mechanical puppets), Westerntown (with a show) and much else besides.

*Praetorium   M9 (M25)

Location
Kleine Budengasse

U-Bahn
Dom/Hauptbahnhof

Buses
132, 133

Trams
5, 9, 11, 12, 16

Opening times
Tues.–Sun. 10 a.m.–5 p.m.

Roman foundations were first discovered on this site in 1570, but it was only in 1953, after wartime destruction in the old town of Cologne, that systematic excavation could begin. An area some 180 m/200 yds square has now been explored, though only a small part of this is accessible.

The building was probably first used as the headquarters of the commander of the Roman army in Lower Germany; then in the second half of the 1st c. it became the Praetorium, the seat of the governor of Lower Germany. Down to the 4th c. a sequence of four building phases has been identified. After the Roman withdrawal the building was occupied until the 7th c. by the Merovingian kings. From the 10th c. until the destruction of the ghetto in 1349 this was the Jewish quarter of Cologne, as the *mikvah* (see Town Hall) still bears witness. The site is an interesting example of historical continuity, with a tradition as the headquarters of authority going back two thousand years: a tradition maintained by the Town Hall, originally built not later than the 12th c. a little way east of the section of the Praetorium now open to the public.

The Roman complex consisted of a palace with large and handsome rooms, the Aula Regia (law court), administrative offices and residential accommodation. Surprisingly, it was set at an angle to the line of the town walls (the foundations of which can be seen outside the east side of the building).

Exhibition

A room at the entrance to the site contains an interesting exhibition of material recovered during the excavations, including small objects of considerable artistic quality, glass and (on the west wall) bricks stamped with the name of a legion – showing that in time of peace the Roman forces devoted themselves to the useful activity of producing building materials. A series of displays illustrate the probable appearance of the building.

Roman drain

From the exhibition room visitors can explore a short section of a Roman drain under Budengasse. With a total length of 140 m/150 yds, it is over 2 m/6½ ft high and 1 m/40 in. wide.

Rathenauplatz

See Synagogue

Rautenstrauch-Joest Museum (Museum of Ethnology)   O10

The Museum of Ethnology (Museum für Völkerkunde) originated in donations by the Rautenstrauch and Joest families (1901), and was housed in a neo-Baroque building by E. Crones (1904–06), which, with the College of Engineering (by Schilling, 1902–04) at Ubierring 48 and a number of well preserved houses in the same street, still conveys something of the atmosphere of Cologne's "Rings" (see entry) in the prosperous years at the end of the 19th c.

The collection is particularly strong in the Pre-Columbian cultures of America, the cultures of the American Indians, Oceania and Africa. There are regular exhibitions on special themes, some of them organised by the Institute of Ethnology of Cologne University.

In the same building is the municipal Little Theatre (Kammer-spiele).

Location
Ubierring 45

Trams
15, 16

Opening times
Tues.–Sun. 10 a.m.–5 p.m.;
1st Wed. in month
10 a.m.–8 p.m.

Conducted tours
Sun. at 3 p.m. and by
arrangement
(tel. 31 10 65/6)

Rhinepark (Rhine Park)

See Trade Fair Grounds and Rheinpark

**Rheinvorstadt   M/N9/10 (L/M/N26)

The historic name of Rheinvorstadt (Rhine suburb) refers to the area between the old Roman walls, running to the west of the Heumarkt and Old Market, and the Rhine, from the street called Filzengraben in the south to the Hohenzollern Bridge in the north. In Roman times there was an arm of the Rhine here (roughly on the line of the Heumarkt and the Old Market) which was used as a harbour, the outer strip of land being occupied by warehouses (see Great St Martin's Church).

In this area there grew up in the Middle Ages one of the principal nuclei of the city. The larger ships which came up the Rhine from the coastal region had to tranship their cargoes here on to vessels of shallower draught which then carried the goods farther upstream. The town profited from this by requiring that all goods so transhipped must first be exposed for sale in Cologne. The first formal confirmation of this right of "staple" was given by Archbishop Konrad von Hochstaden in 1259 and reaffirmed by the Emperor Charles IV in 1349. From the earliest times, therefore, merchants and traders established themselves in this area, using the silted-up Roman harbour for the storage and selling of their wares. In consequence the first extension of the town in the mid 10th c. brought the Rheinvorstadt within the walls, and the foundation of the Benedictine abbey of Great St Martin's (see entry) in the same century gave the area its ecclesiastical centre. The marshy area of the old Roman harbour was drained; and a 12th c. document

U-Bahn
Dom/Hauptbahnhof

Buses
132, 133

Trams
5, 9, 11, 12, 16; or
(Heumarkt) 1, 2, 7

referring to the drainage of one of the last sections of the area by the guild of linen-weavers, with the first known use of the municipal seal, gives the earliest evidence that the town had achieved some degree of self-government.

This new commercial centre promoted the development of a new middle class, sufficiently strong by the year 1074 to rise in revolt against Archbishop Anno II, their ecclesiastical and secular lord. On this occasion the rebellion was suppressed, but the archbishop's authority had been shaken. Thereafter he was compelled to grant the town ever greater concessions (including the right of fortification and the right of staple), and in 1288 he was actually driven out of Cologne.

The patricians who now became rulers of the city, although as merchants they were frequently on the side of the burghers (see Overstolz House), were in turn unable to assert their authority over the burghers, who now organised themselves in craft guilds. After the 1396 rising the city's new constitution provided that political power was to rest in the hands of the whole body of burghers, organised in their various guilds. The tower of the Town Hall (see entry) was now built – a proud symbol of the independence and confidence of the citizens of this quarter with its long traditions.

The Rheinvorstadt continued into modern times to be the commercial quarter of the city, and in spite of the ravages of the Second World War and modern traffic planning it has preserved much of the atmosphere of old Cologne.

Old Market

The Old Market (Alter Markt) is still one of the most character-ful squares in Cologne, although few of the original build-ings have survived. Apart from the tower of the Town Hall perhaps the most notable feature is the double building at Nos. 20–22 ("Zur Brezel" and "Zum Dorn") with its handsome gables.

"Kallendresser"

High up on the wall of No. 24 can be seen the "Kallendresser", a figure (by Ewald Mataré, modelled on an older relief) in a somewhat disrespectful attitude. Although the direct meaning is clear, there are divergent views on the story behind this figure. One explanation is that the burghers of Cologne chose this way of expressing their views to the patrician municipal council (or alternatively to the abbot of Great St Martin's). At any rate figures of this kind have a long tradition: there are some other good examples on the Town Hall tower.

Jan von Werth Fountain

In the centre of the square is the Jan von Werth Fountain (by Wilhelm Albermann, 1884). Jan von Werth was a successful cavalry general in the Thirty Years War. According to an old Cologne legend Jan, a peasant's son, courted a girl named Griet but was rejected as being too poor. Thereupon he went off and rose to fame and fortune. Riding proudly back to Cologne he met Griet, who was still poor, and said: "Well, Griet, if only you had married me!" Whereupon Griet gave the answer of a matter-of-fact Cologne girl: "If only I had known!"

Jan von Werth is still remembered at Carnival time, when his cavalry troop plays a part in the festivities. The Old Market features prominently in the Carnival: it is the starting-point, on the Thursday before Carnival weekend, of the Women's Carnival (Wieverfastelovend or Weiberfastnacht) – an event which even male visitors will find worth observing.

The "Kallendresser" in the Old Market

A junk market is held in the Old Market and the adjoining Martinsviertel on the third Saturday of the month (in summer).

The Martinsviertel (St Martin's quarter), to the east of the Old Market, is the real old town of Cologne, an area famed for its view of the Rhine and which is now an entertainment and residential quarter, closed to motor traffic.

Martinsviertel

The medieval street pattern has largely been preserved, and the new buildings which have been inserted among the old, such as Joachim Schürmann's flats (1975–78) to the north and west of Great St Martin's Church, seek to maintain the character of the district, for example by using the old gable forms.

In the square at the west end of Great St Martin's are monuments to characteristic Cologne types. Tünnes and Schäl (see Notable Personalities) are represented between the seats of a pavement café, and a little farther along is the Schmitz Column (partly built of Roman stones from the town walls), commemorating Ubian (i.e. Cologne) girls, the first moon landing and the noble Cologne family of Schmitz (the city's commonest name), a fit monument for a city which owed its rise to greatness in medieval times not to some prince or other ruler but to its own citizens.

A stroll through the Martinsviertel will reveal many handsome old house fronts and picturesque nooks and corners. On many houses can be seen the booms of the derricks used to hoist goods up to the store-rooms on the upper floors and the mask-like abutments used in the construction of the derricks. It will also be seen, however, that the character of the quarter is being threatened by an influx of restaurants and up-market shops – partly a consequence of high land costs and rents, which have risen beyond the means of ordinary Cologne residents.

Ostermannplatz

To the south, just beyond Lintgasse, is Ostermannplatz, a square created in the 1930s after the demolition of older property. The square is named after Willi Ostermann (1876–1936), a popular writer of Carnival songs. The fountain in the centre (1938) also bears his name; it is decorated with figures from his songs.

At Salzgasse 13 is a notable old house, "Im Walfisch" (1626). From this street either Halbmondgasse or Fassbindergasse will lead into the Eisenmarkt (Iron Market), with the Hännesje Theatre (see Practical Information, Puppet Theatre). From the street called An dem Rothenberg there is a fine view, past a number of old house fronts, of Great St Martin's Church. Nearer the Rhine is another interesting old house, Haus Delft (1620; Am Buttermarkt 42 and Frankenwerft 27).

Immediately east of Great St Martin's is the attractive Fish Market (Fischmarkt). On the wall of Mauthgasse 9 can be seen a plaque commemorating the democratic politician Robert Blum, born here in 1807, who was shot in 1848.

Between Mauthgasse and Frankenwerft stands the 16th c. Stapelhaus, rebuilt after the last war. It was in staple-houses of this kind that all goods transported on the Rhine were required to be exposed for sale for three days.

At Mühlengasse 1–15 is the Brügelmannhaus (1895), the only industrial building still preserved in the city centre. It is planned to house the Theatre Museum in this building.

On the north side of Bischofsgasse are the new premises of the Wallraf–Richartz Museum and Ludwig Museum (see entry), a complex of exhibition rooms and concert halls, which in spite of some interesting architectural features has been criticised for a monumentality inconsistent with the character of the area. There has also been controversy over its cost.

Heumarkt
(Haymarket)

The original pattern of this square, which was surrounded by the handsome houses of wealthy merchant families, suffered from the heavy destruction of the Second World War, and has finally been destroyed by modern schemes of traffic management. One notable house which has survived, however, can be seen at No. 77 ("Zum St Peter", 16th c.).

Rheingasse and
Filzengraben

Here too there has been much destruction of the original structure. At the corner of Malzbüchel and Paradiesgasse the old-established Malzmühle brewery has a fine old drinking saloon. In the street called Am Thurnmarkt, on the banks of the Rhine, is a small gate in the old town walls. In Rheingasse is the handsome old Overstolz House (see entry).

In Filzengraben (on the line of the old walls) stands the Church of the Trinity (see entry), built by Protestants who settled in this area in the 19th c. Other features of interest are the church of St Mary's in Lyskirchen (see entry) and the monument of the Ubii on the Roman walls (see entry).

Richmodis House

See Neumarkt

The "Rings" and Neustadt   L10–O10 (K24–O23)

The "Rings" are the boulevards which run in a semicircle round the old town, laid out (architect, Hermann Joseph Stübben) from 1881 onwards after the demolition of the Romanesque town walls (see entry). Originally they had villas and public buildings set among gardens and also some residential areas, but later were more closely built up.

Few of the older buildings survived the last war; among those which did were the Rautenstrauch-Joest Museum (see entry) on the Ubierring and the neo-Gothic Hansagymnasium (a grammar school) on the Hansaring. Another building which survived was Cologne's first tower block, also on the Hansaring, built by Hans Koerfer in 1924, when it was the highest such block in Europe. The medieval gate towers were incorporated in the layout of the Rings (see Romanesque town walls).

The Rings are now busy commercial streets with heavy traffic, though there are plans, inevitably controversial, to restore sections of them to their original character as boulevards. The names of the various streets reflect the history of Germany and of Cologne, from the Ubierring in the south to the Theodor-Heuss-Ring in the north.

Neustadt, Cologne's "New Town", was built on the area outside the walls which had previously been kept clear of all building to provide a free field of fire. Some handsome buildings have survived from period of prosperity in the late 19th c., for example in the Südstadt area (east of the Bonner Strasse), around the Volksgarten (see entry), in Rathenauplatz (see Synagogue), near the Stadtgarten (see entry) and in the neighbourhood of St Agnes's Church (see entry). The outer limit of Neustadt was marked by the city's new fortifications on the line of the Inner Green Belt (see entry).

Location
Ubierring to Theodor-Heuss-Ring and farther out

Trams
6, (10), 15, (16)

Neustadt

Roman aqueduct   M9 (L25)

Remarkable evidence of the engineering skill of the Romans is provided by the remains of their aqueducts. As early as the 1st c. water was already being brought to Cologne from some 10 km/6 miles away, and in the 2nd c. a 90 km/55 mile long aqueduct was constructed to carry water from the Eifel hills (tapping the source of the river Urft, near Nettersheim/Mechernich to the SW of Cologne). Skilful use was made of the fall from 420 m/1380 ft to 50 m/165 ft, valleys being spanned by aqueducts, hills pierced by tunnels. The flow of water to Cologne is estimated to have been about 200 litres/88 gallons per second. The system remained in use until the end of the Roman period and then fell into disrepair.

In the Middle Ages the remains of the aqueduct were regarded as a work of the devil and became known as the Devil's Ditch. There is an old legend that the architect of Cologne Cathedral, Master Gerhard, made a wager with the devil that he would complete the cathedral before the devil could bring water to the site. The devil, it is said, won the wager by making use of the Roman aqueduct, whereupon Gerhard flung himself to his death from the scaffolding of the cathedral.

Location
In a small park at the corner of Drususgasse and An der Rechtschule

U-Bahn
Dom/Hauptbahnhof

Buses
132, 133

Trams
5, 9, 11, 12, 16

A small section of the aqueduct has been set up at the north-west corner of the Wallraf-Richartz Museum (see entry).

**Romanesque town walls between L10 and O10 (K24 and O3)
(Romanische Stadtmauer)

The new settlements of merchants and traders and the building of religious houses had made it necessary for Cologne to extend its boundaries beyond the old Roman walls (see entry) on several occasions before 1180, when, against the wishes of Archbishop Philipp von Heinsberg, the citizens of the town asserted their right to build new town walls. The right of fortification, which the Emperor Henry IV had previously granted to the burghers of Cologne (or, to be more precise, to the patrician municipal council) in 1106 was one of the first privileges which they were able to wring out of the archbishop, their ruler.

The circuit of walls, 5·5 km/3½ miles long, ran just inside the line of the present Rings (see entry), their course still marked by such street names as Severinswall, Kartäuserwall and Pantaleonswall. Twelve large fortified gateways (the same number as in the heavenly Jerusalem of the Book of Revelation: the secular city as the image of the celestial one) and a number of smaller gates gave entrance to the town. In terms of area Cologne was now the largest city in Germany, and there was still some arable land within the walls until the 19th c.: it was

The Eigelstein Gate, a relic of the medieval town walls

only in the industrial age that the town filled up the walled area and began to expand beyond the walls (from a population of 49,000 in 1816 Cologne had increased to 144,772 by 1880). In 1881 the city bought the walls from the state for 12 million marks and began to pull them down (see Rings).

A number of the old gates and sections of the walls have survived, incorporated into the new street pattern. The following are the most important.

The name Weckschnapp (from *wecken*, a bread roll, and *schnappen*, to snatch) of this tower, now built into a house, recalls a gruesome story of a medieval prison (though the prison in question was not in this tower but in another one now destroyed). The prisoners were left without food apart from a roll which was suspended from the ceiling of their cell. When they jumped up to snatch the roll they inevitably fell through a hole in the floor and were cut to pieces on knives which were set up beneath.

Weckschnapp, Konrad-Adenauer-Ufer 69

The Eigelstein Gate, a central feature of the Eigelstein quarter (see entry), now stands in a pedestrian precinct. On the inner side of the gate, in a recess at the east end, hangs a lifeboat from the cruiser "Köln", which was sunk in the First World War; at the west end is a figure of the Cologne peasant (1885), recalling Cologne's status since 1475 (though only in heraldry!) as leader of the peasants of the Empire. The Cologne peasant features in the annual Carnival.

Eigelsteintor (Eigelstein Gate), Am Eigelstein

This tower ("St Gereon's Mill Tower") was built in the 15th c. It gives a good impression of the massiveness of the walls.

Gereonsmühlenturm, Hansaring

The Hahnentor ("Cock's Gate") is the most richly decorated of the gates, since it was the gate by which the German king entered after being crowned in Aachen. The king was required to go to Cologne immediately after his coronation in order to take his seat in the cathedral chapter and pay homage to the Three Kings (see Cathedral). The upper floors of the tower are now used for exhibitions.

Hahnentor, Rudolfplatz

On the outside of the section of wall to the west of the Ulre Gate is the oldest secular memorial tablet in Germany (1360). It marks the occasion when, during the conflict between Archbishop Engelbert von Falkenburg and the burghers of Cologne, the archbishop's forces sought to enter the town with the help of a local cobbler whom they had suborned but were repulsed by the citizens under the leadership of the patrician merchant Mathias Overstolz.

Of the Ulre Gate, originally a double gateway with towers, there survives only one tower, which was converted into a windmill in the 15th c. It is now the headquarters of the "Red Sparks" (Rote Funken), a Carnival association formed in 1823 which is an ironical revival of the old town guard.

Ulrepforte (Ulre Gate)

This handsome gate tower stands in the centre of Chlodwig-platz. The rooms in the interior are now used for various public occasions.

Severinstorburg (St Severinus's Gate), Chlodwigplatz

The Bottmühle is one of the four windmills built on the town walls (16th c.).

Bottmühle, An der Bottmühle

Roman fort

Bayenturm, Am Bayenturm   The Bayenturm was the most southerly corner tower on the banks of the Rhine, probably with outworks reaching out into the river. The upper floors, destroyed during the war, have not yet been restored.

Roman fort   M10 (M27)

Location
Urbanstrasse

Trams
1, 2, 7

About 310 the Emperor Constantine caused the first bridge to be constructed over the Rhine, the frontier between the Roman Empire and the territory of the Germans, together with a military camp or fort some 141 m/463 ft square. Of the fort there survive the walls of the east gate with its semicircular towers, to the north of the Lufthansa building, on th footpath to Old St Heribert's (see entry), and the remains of the central tower on the north side (to the west of Old St Heribert's). After the Romans left, the fort became from the 5th c. a royal stronghold of the Frankish kings. About the year 1000 the Emperor Otto III presented the site to Archbishop Heribert, who thereupon began to build Old St Heribert's Abbey.

**Roman-Germanic Museum   M9 (L25)
(Römisch-Germanisches Museum)

Location
Roncalliplatz 4

U-Bahn
Dom/Hauptbahnhof

Buses
132, 133

Trams
5, 9, 11, 12, 16

Opening times
Tues. and Fri.–Sun.
10 a.m.–5 p.m.,
Wed. and Thurs.
10 a.m.–8 p.m.

Conducted tours
Sun. at 11.30 a.m. and by
arrangement
(tel. 2 21 44 38)

Interest in the remains of antiquity was first aroused in the 16th c. under the influence of humanism, and the first collections of Roman material came into being. The earliest display of Roman finds was in the Wallraf-Richartz Museum (see entry) in 1861.

The number of finds increased during the 19th c. as a result of excavation for building developments in the rapidly growing city, but systematic archaeological investigation began only in 1914, under the Prussian law on excavation. Of the many archaeologists who have since been involved, the name of Otto Doppelfeld merits special mention as that of the man who has made perhaps the greatest contribution to the archaeology of Cologne.

The Roman-Germanic Museum was founded in 1946, and the present museum building was begun in 1967 and opened in 1974. Designed by Hugo Borger, it sets an exemplary standard in the display and explanation of its material. An extensive audio-visual system provides full information on the exhibits, illustrating through them the various aspects of Roman and Germanic culture.

The following exhibits are of particular interest.

Dionysus Mosaic

From the staircase visitors can look down on the famous Dionysus Mosaic, discovered here in 1941 during the construction of an underground air-raid shelter. Albertus Magnus had already referred in the 13th c. to the "magnificent floors of the pagan period" which he had seen while visiting the cathedral building site.

The mosaic covered the floor of a room in a peristyle house (i.e. a house with an inner courtyard and colonnade) of the 1st–3rd c. which had a total area of 40 m/130 ft by 65 m/213 ft,

Tomb of Poblicius ▶

Roman-Germanic Museum

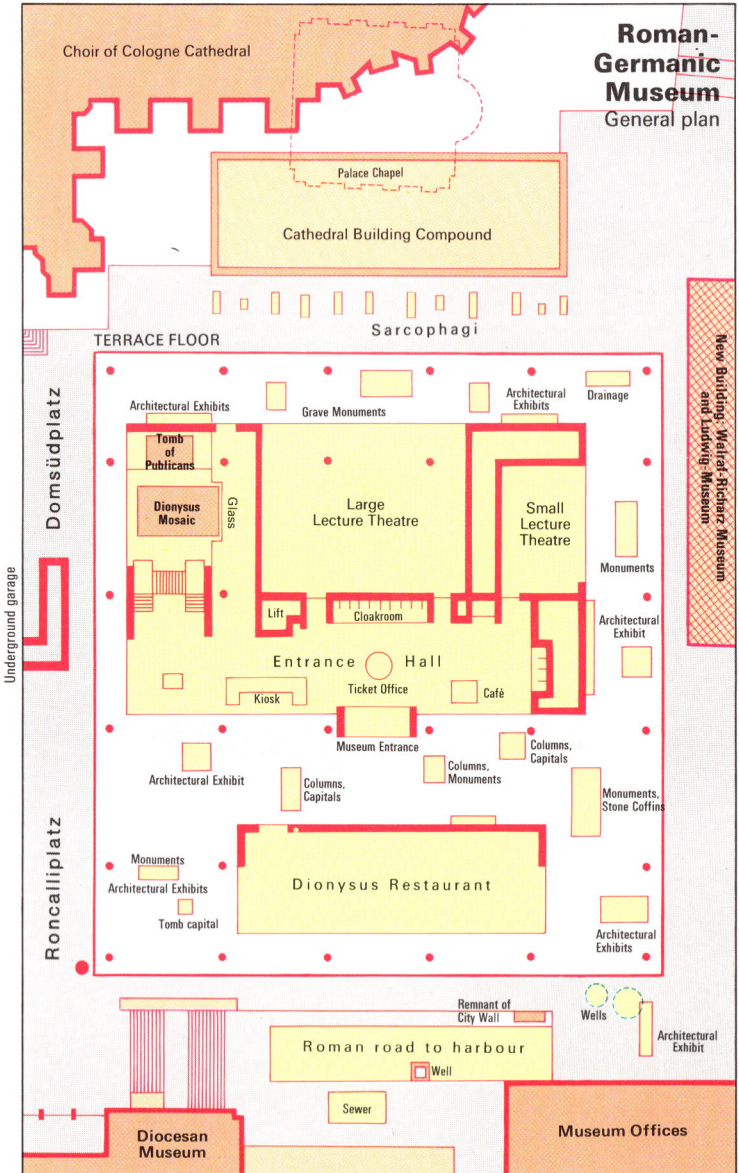

Roman-Germanic Museum
General plan

Choir of Cologne Cathedral

Palace Chapel

Cathedral Building Compound

Sarcophagi

New Building, Wallraf-Richartz-Museum and Ludwig-Museum

TERRACE FLOOR

Domsüdplatz

Underground garage

Roncalliplatz

Architectural Exhibits

Tomb of Publicans

Dionysus Mosaic

Glass

Grave Monuments

Architectural Exhibits

Drainage

Large Lecture Theatre

Small Lecture Theatre

Monuments

Lift

Cloakroom

Architectural Exhibit

Entrance Hall

Kiosk

Ticket Office

Café

Museum Entrance

Architectural Exhibit

Columns, Capitals

Columns, Monuments

Columns, Capitals

Monuments, Stone Coffins

Monuments

Architectural Exhibits

Tomb capital

Dionysus Restaurant

Architectural Exhibits

Remnant of City Wall

Wells

Roman road to harbour

Well

Architectural Exhibit

Sewer

Diocesan Museum

Museum Offices

Source: Römisch-Germanisches Museum, Köln

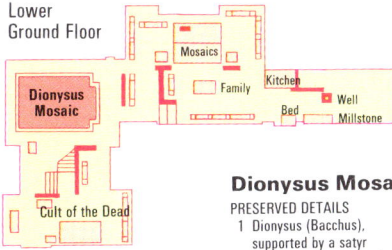

Lower Ground Floor

Roman-Germanic Museum

Dionysus Mosaic

PRESERVED DETAILS
1 Dionysus (Bacchus), supported by a satyr
2 Maenad (with lyre) and satyr (with flute)
3 Pair of dancers (damaged)
4 Satyr and Maenad (with tambourine)
5 Eros on a lion

6 Invitation to the dance
7 Satyr family
8 Silen on an ass
9 Satyr playing a flute
10 Pan with a goat
11 Panther
12 Ducks
13 Cantharus with birds
14 Pears in a cantharas
15 Fox

16 Birds pulling a cart filled with fruits
17 Figs on a branch
18 Birds pulling a cart with harvest tools
19 Cherries in a woven basket
20 Peacock holding a pear in its beak
21 Shells

Main Floor

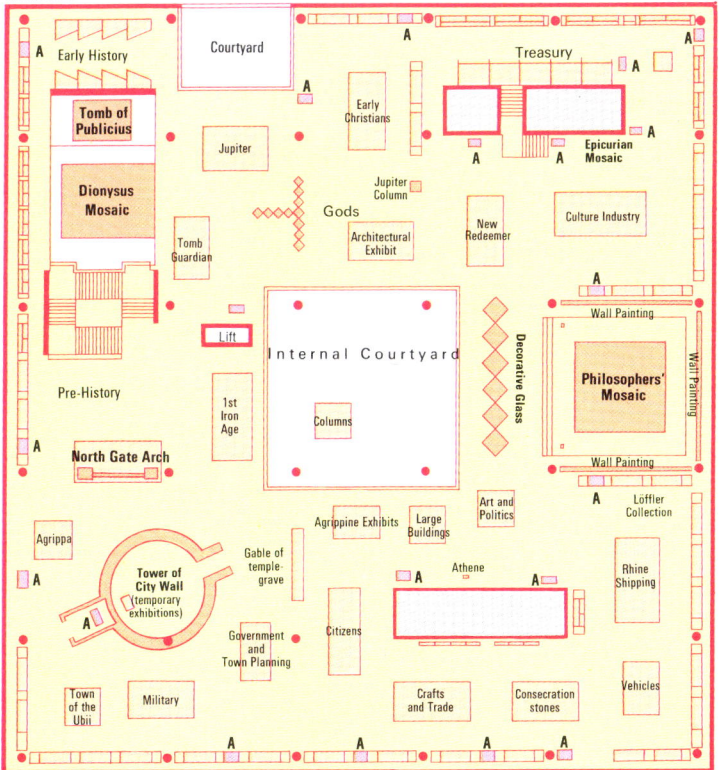

Source: Römisch-Germanisches Museum, Köln

A scene from the Doinysus Mosaic

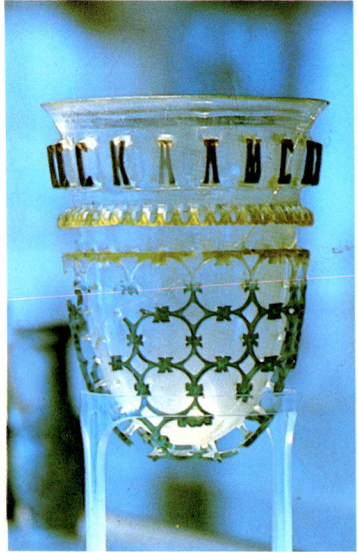

A "cage-cup"

or about the same as the present museum. It depicts dancing scenes, figures, fruits and animals associated with the cult of Dionysus, god of wine and of vegetation, who is seen in the central panel leaning drunkenly on a satyr from his train. It is not known whether the room was used for riotous parties, in a kind of secular homage to Dionysus, or for the celebration of an orgiastic cult.

Tomb of Poblicius

Above the mosaic rears the imposing tomb of Poblicius, which was discovered in 1967 during excavation work in Chlodwig-platz (see Severinsviertel) and purchased by the city in 1970. The restored parts can be distinguished from the original by their lighter colour. The monument, 14·6 m/48 ft high, was erected about 40 A.D. by Poblicius (named in the inscription on the front), who was evidently a very wealthy man, to serve as his tomb. Poblicius himself stands between two other figures (members of his family?) on the upper storey of the monument, flanked by Corinthian columns. From the galleries on either side there is a good view of his interesting profile and of reliefs of scenes from the cult of Dionysus, here representing eternal life and bliss.

Lower floor

On the lower floor are exhibits illustrating the Roman cult of the dead and a room devoted to everyday life in Roman times, with domestic pottery, furniture, games, etc.

Ground floor gallery

Glass from the Eastern Mediterranean, including two glass chains of about 1300 B.C. from Mycenae (Greece).

Upper floor

Objects of the prehistoric and early historical periods found in

Cologne (from the Palaeolithic period, *c.* 100,000 B.C. to the early centuries A.D. – non-Roman material only).

The arch of the north gate of the Roman town (see Roman walls), on the south side of the staircase, marks the beginning of the Roman period. The letters CCAA give the name of Roman Cologne and summarise the story of its origin: C(olonia), a settlement governed by Roman law; C(laudia), founded in the reign of the Emperor Claudius; A(ra), with an altar of the imperial cult; A(grippinensium), established at the wish of Agrippina, Claudius's wife, a native of Cologne who secured the grant of municipal status for her town.
Just beyond the North Gate is a reconstruction of a Roman tower (the Lysolph Tower), which is used to accommodate small special exhibitions.

North Gate

Of the material illustrating different aspects of Roman life which is displayed on island sites and in cases, only a brief selection can be mentioned:
portrait of Agrippa, Agrippina's grandfather, who founded Cologne in 38 B.C. by settling the Ubii here (island 102);
portrait of the Emperor Augustus (island 102);
bust of Agrippina (island 105);
a small female figure with features of a type which can still be seen in Cologne (case 13);
masks of river gods (island 118);
reconstruction of a Roman travelling carriage (island 119).
Roman glass is displayed in cases 28 to 31B. Of particular interest is a "cage-cup" (*diatreton*), enclosed in a network of raised ornament, with the Greek inscription "Drink, enjoy life for ever". Such fine vessels as this are believed to have been produced only in Cologne.

Material from Roman Cologne

The small room adjoining the display of glass contains the 3rd c. Philosophers Mosaic (with figures of Greek philosophers and poets) and 2nd c. wall paintings.

Philosophers Mosaic

The Treasury (below the Study Gallery) contains jewellery, including non-Roman material; some of it comes from private collections.

Treasury

Bronze articles, coins and pottery lamps.

Study Gallery

**Roman tomb, Weiden

This tomb, constructed in the mid 2nd c. and rediscovered in 1843, is one of the finest of its kind north of the Alps, notable particularly for its excellently preserved furnishings. It belonged to a Roman villa (country estate) which has not been located. Situated 6 m/20 ft below ground level, it reproduces the layout of a Roman dining room: an expression of hope for an agreeable life in the hereafter. Hewn out of the walls are three couches, finely faced with marble, on which the men reclined during a meal, and in the corners are two reproductions in limestone of the wicker chairs on which women sat. On the couches are portrait busts (two women on the south side, a man on the north side). Cut into the walls are small niches for ash-urns (cremation burials).

Location
Aachener Strasse 328,
Cologne-Weiden

Bus
151

Distance
10 km/6 miles W

Opening times
Tues.–Thurs. 10 a.m.–1 p.m.,
Fri. 10 a.m.–5 p.m.,
Sat. and Sun. 1–5 p.m.;
by appointment
(tel. 02234/73399)

The tomb contains a 3rd c. sarcophagus, reflecting a change in burial practice; originally the sarcophagus would not be in the tomb but in a small funerary temple above it. It is carved with a representation of the dead husband and wife in a medallion, flanked by winged figures (personifications of the seasons?) and by smaller scenes.

In a room above the tomb are displayed the grave goods associated with the burial, together with explanatory photographs and diagrams.

Roman tower

See Roman walls

*Roman walls (Römische Stadtmauer)   M9 (L24/25)

In A.D. 50, on the initiative of the Emperor Claudius's wife Agrippina, the *oppidum Ubiorum* (the fortified settlement of the Ubii) was granted the status of a *colonia* governed by Roman law and the style of Colonia Claudia Ara Agrippiniensium, and soon afterwards a beginning was made with the construction of a 3·9 km/2½ mile long circuit of walls. The walls were strengthened by 21 towers and had nine gates. They had an inner and an outer face of hewn stone with a filling of cement-like rubble. The Roman walls continued to bound the city well into the Middle Ages, and it was not until the 10th c. that an extension of the walled area to include the Rheinvorstadt became necessary. There were further extensions on the north and south sides in the 11th c.; then in 1180, with the construction of the Romanesque town walls (see entry), the Roman walls were pulled down.

Remains of the walls can be seen at many points in the city. The most important are described below.

North Gate
Komödienstrasse/Domplatte
Buses: 132, 133
Trams: 5, 9, 11, 12, 16

The Roman North Gate stood in the street called An der Burgmauer, roughly opposite the Tourist Office. It had three openings, a central passage 5·60 m/18 ft wide and 8·60 m/28 ft high (arch now in the Roman-Germanic Museum) and two lateral openings 1·90 m/6 ft wide; the one on the east side now stands at the north-west corner of the Domplatte, near its original site. In the 12th c. the gate was converted into a house for the dean of the cathedral and in this condition survived until 1826, when the central archway was demolished. In 1892 the whole structure was pulled down. The eastern arch was re-erected in its present position in 1971.

Fragment of wall in
Cathedral car park

Near the Trankgasse entrance to the Cathedral underground car park a good section of the wall can be seen. There are other remains (not accessible) farther east under the foundations of the Cathedral.

Lysolph Tower (Lysolphturm)
Corner of Komödienstrasse
and Tunisstrasse
Trams: 3, 4, 5, 9, 11, 12, 16

The name of the tower dates from the Middle Ages, when it was occupied by the Lysolph family. It was exposed and consolidated during work on the construction of the U-Bahn. The masonry is excellently preserved.

Interior of the Roman tomb at Weiden

Severinstorburg (St Severinus's Gate)

The Roman Tower

Section of wall at Arsenal An der Burgmauer	The core of the Arsenal (see entry) wall on the street called An der Burgmauer is Roman (not visible). The so-called Roman Fountain preserves the form of a Roman tower (to east of Arsenal); on its walls are portraits of Roman emperors and an inscription from Tacitus's *Annals* which refers – unfortunately in fragmentary form – to Cologne. The wall to the west of the Arsenal is Roman.
Roman Tower (Römerturm) At corner of Zeughausstrasse and St-Apern-Strasse	This is the best preserved of Cologne's Roman towers, widely famed for its excellent condition. In the Middle Ages it was incorporated in the convent of Poor Clares (now destroyed), serving as privies. In 1873, when it formed part of a dwelling-house, it was in danger of demolition, but was then bought by the city for 19,000 thalers and restored; its battlements date from this period. The outer wall, 2·5 m/8 ft thick, still preserves much of its red-and-white Roman ornament.
Helenenturm (Helen's Tower) At corner of St-Apern- Strasse and Helenenstrasse	This is believed to have been the only half-tower (open on the inner side) on the Roman walls.
Fragment of wall on Mauritiussteinweg	Between No. 41 and 43 Mauritiussteinweg (to the east, behind the houses) is a 140 m/150 yd long stretch of wall, formerly built into later houses.
Fragments of wall on the line of the Duffesbach	The street-names Rothgerberbach, Blaubach and Mühlenbach mark the course (now underground) of the Duffesbach, a stream the higher north bank of which offered a good line for the walls on the south side of the town. All along this stretch there are remains of walls and towers, and the course of the old Roman wall is marked by modern brick walls. The names Rothgerberbach and Blaubach reflect the fact that tanners (*gerber*) and dyers (*blau*=dye) were established here in medieval times.
Monument of the Ubii (Ubiermonument) Buses: 132, 133 Trams: 1, 2, 7	The basement of Malzmühle 1 can be visited by arrangement with the Roman-Germanic Museum (see entry). The name of this feature is based on the assumption that the square tower on this site dates from the time of the *oppidum Ubiorum*. Examination of timber from the foundations set in the gravel soil of what was formerly the bank of the Rhine, using the most modern archaeological techniques, has shown that the trees were felled in the year A.D. 4. At any rate the tower is the earliest Roman wall-tower north of the Alps. In addition to the remains of the tower there is a small exhibition displaying much Roman material found in the surrounding area.

Sacred Heart, Church of the

See Herz-Jesu-Kirche

St Agnes's Church   K9

Location Neusser Platz	This neo-Gothic church by Carl Rüdell and Richard Odenthal (1896–1902) was built by Peter Joseph Roeckerath in memory

of his wife Agnes. Its spire, richly decorated with tracery, looks directly down Neusser Strasse to the Eigelstein Gate in the Romanesque town walls (see entry).

In the surrounding area, particularly between Neusser Strasse and Riehler Strasse, there are still some handsome late 19th c. house-fronts to be seen.

U-Bahn
Ebertplatz

Trams
5, 6, 9, 10, 11, 12, 15, 16

*St Andrew's Church (St Andreas) M9 (L25)

This Dominican church combines in charming juxtaposition the Late Romanesque architecture of the Rhineland with High Gothic in the French tradition. The first monastic church on this site, then outside the (Roman) town walls, was built in the 10th c. at the behest of Archbishop Bruno I. The original choir was preserved in a rebuilding of 1200, but gave place in 1414 to its Gothic successor. The church reached its present form with the rebuilding of the transverse choirs in the 15th c. Post-war restoration work somewhat altered the original aspect of the church, making the roof flatter than it had previously been.

Location
Andreaskloster

U-Bahn
Dom/Hauptbahnhof

Buses
132, 133

Trams
5, 9, 11, 12, 16

The finest view of the church is to be had from Komödienstrasse or the north side of the Cathedral. The octagonal Romanesque tower over the Gothic choir is the most striking feature in the neighbourhood of the Cathedral. The massive west front dominates the Romanesque nave.

Exterior

The porch at the west end is a masterly example of the Late Romanesque style of the Rhineland. The low nave with the Romanesque articulation of its walls, emphasising the horizontals (fine ornamental capitals and frieze of foliage), is followed by the dome over the crossing, which – its form adjusted to the original 10th c. choir – comes lower down than the vaulting of the nave. The adjoining high choir, modelled on the Sainte Chapelle in Paris (or on the choir of the Coronation Chapel in Aachen), has walls almost wholly dissolved into windows. In characteristically Gothic fashion the verticals are here dominant, particularly in the engaged columns between the windows with their fine figural consoles in the "soft style" of 1420. The transverse choirs are also Gothic. The side chapels in the aisles are 14th c.

Interior

On the west side of the porch is a 15th c. reliquary over which the blood of St Ursula and her companions is said to have flowed during their martyrdom.

In the south-western chapel is the Altarpiece of the Brother-hood of the Rosary, by the Master of St Severinus (c. 1500). Painted in thanksgiving for the victory over Charles the Bold, it documents the foundation of the Brotherhood by Jacob Sprenger, the Dominican prior who was one of the authors of the "Malleus Maleficarum" ("Hammer of the Witches"), the great textbook of the witch-hunts in Europe. Sprenger is depicted, wearing a black hat, on the left in the foreground of the painting. To the left, at the feet of the Virgin, is Pope Sixtus IV; to the right is the Emperor Frederick III. In the south-east chapel are 14th c. wall paintings (east wall, Christ as Judge of the world; west wall, Coronation of the Virgin).

On the south-west pier of the crossing is a 15th c. Madonna of the Rosary.

Furnishings

St Cecilia's Church

Interior of St Andrew's Church

Reliquary of the Maccabees

In the south choir is the Reliquary of the Maccabees, a magnificent example of Cologne goldsmiths' work (1527).

At the south-east pier of the crossing a staircase leads down to the crypt (a postwar structure built in the remains of a 10th c. crypt). A Roman sarcophagus in the crypt contains the remains of Albertus Magnus (see Notable Personalities), a man of universal learning and one of the leading theologians and philosophers of the Middle Ages.

In the high choir are fine choir-stalls of 1420 and a 16th c. winged altarpiece by B. Bruyn the Elder.

In the north choir are a "Crucifixion of St Andrew" (1658) and a triptych of the Resurrection (16th c.).

On the north-west pier of the crossing is a figure of St Michael (15th c.).

The north-west chapel has well preserved Gothic wall paintings (on the east wall, scenes from the life of the Virgin).

St Cecilia's Church (St Cäcilien)

See Schnütgen Museum

*St Cunibert's Church (St Kunibert)   L10 (K26)

Location
Kunibertskloster 6

Bishop Cunibert of Cologne is said to have built a church dedicated to St Clement in the 7th c., but no trace of such a building has yet been found. Cunibert himself was canonised

St Ursula

Life of St Cunibert

in 1168, and in 1247 the last large church of the Hohenstaufen period before the Cathedral, and the most uniform in style, was dedicated to him. The west end of the church, with its tower, has not yet been rebuilt after its wartime destruction, but the restoration of the rest of the church has been completed.

The choir of St Cunibert's with its two east towers is the most striking feature on the skyline of the northern section of Cologne's Rhine embankment. A feature, characteristic of the choirs of churches of the Hohenstaufen period in Cologne, is the double tier of windows with a dwarf gallery round the top. The proportions of the sides are upset by the absence of the west end; but even without the west end the interior of the church is of imposing dimensions (height 24 m/79 ft, length including west end 62 m/203 ft). The church's mature Romanesque forms, discreetly enhanced by painting, give the interior a firm articulation. The two-tier design of the exterior of the choir is repeated in the interior.

In the south aisle are two bells from the destroyed west tower, St Cunibert's Bell and St Clement's (1773).
Against one of the piers bearing the arcade stands an altar of the Crucifixion (wood, 1500) from Brabant.
Reaching over the crossing is a fine Annunciation, with the Virgin on the south-west pier and the archangel opposite her on the north-west pier. The two figures (1439), of outstanding quality, were probably the work of Konrad Kuyn, master of works of the Cathedral; the donor was Canon Hermanus de Arc- ka, who is depicted as a small figure kneeling at the Virgin's feet. In the south transept, in a niche with 13th c. wall paintings, is a Romanesque font.

U-Bahn
Breslauer Platz

Trams
5, 9, 11, 12, 16

Opening times
Throughout the day

Furnishings

The magnificent stained glass in the choir is among the finest Romanesque glass in Germany. In the south transept, below, is depicted John the Baptist; in the apse, below, St Ursula and St Cordula; above, from right to left, scenes from the life of St Cunibert, the Tree of Jesse, with Old and New Testament scenes, and scenes from the life of St Clement; in the north transept, St Cecilia, St Catherine and the Virgin.

On the south wall of the choir is a tabernacle of 1500.

A grille-like slate slab in the floor of the choir conceals a 17 m/ 56 ft deep well dating from pre-Christian times, the water from which was popularly believed to promote fertility in women. In 1933 a room was found under the high altar giving access to the well. It is interesting to find a pre-Christian well of this kind incorporated in a Christian church.

The reliquaries in the apse (19th c.) house wooden medieval sarcophagi containing the remains of St Cunibert and the two SS. Ewald (missionaries and martyrs).

In a niche in the north wall of the choir superb wall paintings of 1250 were discovered after the removal of a wooden chest.

Against one of the piers in the north aisle can be seen a beautiful Madonna of 1500.

St George's Church   N9 (N25)

Location
Georgsplatz 1

Buses
132, 133

Opening times
Throughout the day

The oldest foundations under this church are those of a Roman station on the road to Bonn (on the line of present-day Severinstrasse). Later a Merovingian church was built on the site. In 1059 Archbishop Anno II founded a college of canons and built a basilican church with a roof borne on columns. The church was vaulted in the mid 12th c., and soon afterwards the west choir was begun (but left unfinished). The church has been brought back to its 12th c. form by restoration work, mainly carried out after the last war.

Exterior

The massive undecorated west end of the Hohenstaufen period, facing on to Severinstrasse, closes off the simple nave with its round-headed windows. The church is now entered by the north porch, all that remains of a 16th c. passage linking St George's collegiate church with the parish church of St James to the north (demolished after the secularisation of the college in 1802).

Interior

In the porch note the imposts, with figural decoration, supporting the ribs of the vaulting. In the church itself the most impressive part is the Hohenstaufen west work with the characteristic articulation of the walls. Under the east choir, still essentially in the form in which it was built by Archbishop Anno, is a five-aisled crypt of the 11th c.

Furnishings

In the central apse of the west end is a fine 14th c. forked crucifix and in front of it a 13th c. font. The windows in the west choir and the nave were the work of the Expressionist artist J. Thorn-Prikker (1930). In the south choir chapel is a tabernacle of 1556. In the choir hangs a copy of the magnificent Romanesque cross of 1067 which is now in the Schnütgen Museum (see entry). After the collapse of the vaulting during the Second World War the cross remained hanging from the arch of the apse, which was still standing (photographs in

north aisle). The altarpiece in the apse is by B. Bruyn the Younger (16th c.). A doorway on the west side of the porch leads into a small inner courtyard with the graves of people killed by bombing during the Second World War (design of the courtyard and Stations of the Cross by Thorn-Prikker).
In the square on the north side of the church is the Hermann Joseph Fountain (1894). Legend relates that Hermann Joseph, who lived in the 12th c., presented an apple to the Christ Child in an effigy of the Virgin and Child, who, it is said, accepted the offering.

**St Gereon's Church   L8 (L23/24)

St Gereon's Church, named after the 4th c. martyr who became Cologne's patron saint, is one of the city's oldest churches and one of the most extraordinary buildings in the West, with a dome which is compared with that of Haghia Sophia in Istanbul.
Gereon was a captain in the Theban Legion who was martyred with his fellow-soldiers during the persecution of Christians at the beginning of the 4th c. Later in the century, with the support of the Emperors of the day, the elliptical central part of the present church with its surrounding conches was built over the supposed position of their graves. This was later used for the burial of Frankish and Merovingian kings, and in 818 of the first Archbishop of Cologne, Hildebold (who built the predecessor of the present Cathedral). Associated with the church from the 9th c. was a college of canons, and in the 11th c. Archbishop Anno II built the canons' choir, with a crypt below. The apse at the east end and the tower were built by Archbishop Arnold von Wied in the 12th c., following the model of the church which he had erected at Schwarzrheindorf near Bonn. At the beginning of the 13th c. the Roman central structure was remodelled to form the present Decagon with its vaulted roof, and soon afterwards the baptistery was built on to the south side of the Decagon. The Gothic sacristy was added in the 14th c., probably by the Cathedral workshops. After suffering heavy damage during the Second World War the exterior was restored by 1979; the restoration of the interior was substantially complete by 1983.

The east choir of the Hohenstaufen period stands on the processional way from the Cathedral (on the line of Unter Sachsenhausen and Gereonstrasse); and the special importance of the processional way and St Gereon's Church is shown by the fact that the first Corpus Christi procession in Cologne in 1297 followed this route. The articulation of the exterior is the first example in Cologne of the Hohenstaufen two-storey choir – a model followed by the Church of the Holy Apostles, Great St Martin's and St Cunibert's (see entries). The seven-storey east towers are little lower than the 48 m/157 ft high pyramidal roof of the Decagon. The exterior of the Decagon with its pointed windows and flying buttresses already shows the elements of Early Gothic, but these are still subservient to the tiered horizontal articulation of Romanesque.

The interior of the Decagon is of overwhelming effect. On the

Location
Gereonshof 4

U-Bahn
Appellhofplatz/Zeughaus

Trams
3, 4, 5, 9, 11, 12, 16

Opening times
Throughout the day

Exterior

Interior

St Gereon

Development of the building

Basilica of St Gereon
(former collegiate church)

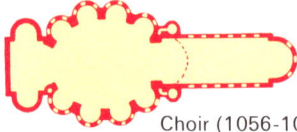

Building under Constantine; 4th c.

Choir (1056-1075) consecrated by Archbishop Anno

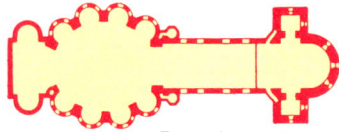

Extension under Archbishop Arnold von Wied (1151-1156)

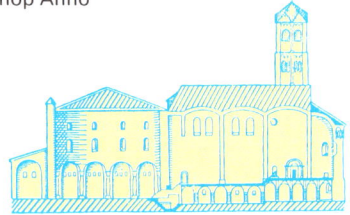

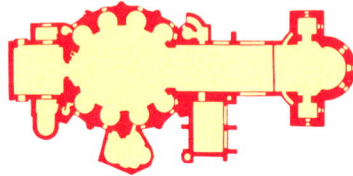

Extensions between 1219 and 1227

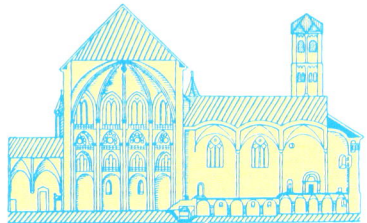

north and south sides the eight conches of the original Roman building are clearly visible, and Roman masonry still forms the core of the structure to a height of 16 m/52 ft. The ribs of the vaulting span a distance of 21 m/69 ft from east to west, meeting at a height of 34 m/112 ft in a wooden boss in the form of a pomegranate.

The red painting of the dome with its gold "Easter drops" dates from 1979, the stained glass by Meistermann and Buschulte from the 1980s. The baptistery has ribbed vaulting of the Hohenstaufen period. The long choir – raised because of the crypt below – has the same two-storey structure as the exterior. The wall paintings (12th c.) in the apse and arcades are badly faded. The sacristy is in the French Gothic style as practised by the Cathedral workshops.

St Gereon's Church ▶

The Decagon . . .

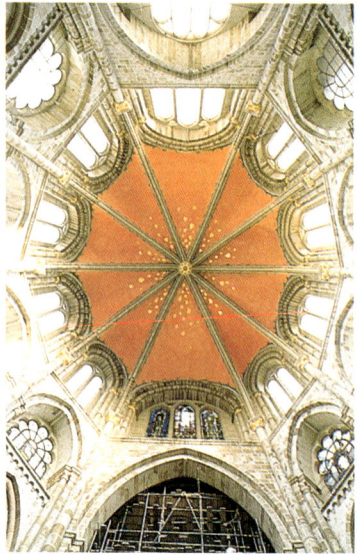

. . . and its dome

Furnishings

Between the Decagon and the high choir is a Baroque altar from St Columba's Church in Cologne.

The beautiful sacristy door in the south wall of the choir is 16th c. work.

The figure of the Virgin on the crescent moon in the choir is 15th c.

On the north wall of the choir can be seen a "Glorification of the Trinity" (1635) with a very interesting view of Cologne in the lower part of the picture.

At the west end of the crypt, in a *confessio* on a lower level, are the Roman martyrs' sarcophagi.

The capitals in the crypt date from the 11th c. (west end) and 12th c. (apse).

The 11th c. mosaic pavement in the apse of the crypt was originally in the high choir; it has representations of Samson and David and the signs of the zodiac. The altar is 16th c.

St Martin's Church

See Great St Martin's Church

St Mary's in the Capitol (St Maria im Kapitol)   M9 (N25)

Location
Kasinostrasse 6

St Mary's in the Capitol, built on the site of a Roman temple of the 1st c. A.D. dedicated to the Capitoline triad of Jupiter, Juno

and Minerva, is the earliest example of the successful combination of a longitudinal nave with the centralised structure of a trilobate choir (see Great St Martin's Church), which was later to be so fruitful in Cologne (Holy Apostles, Great St Martin's – see entries) and elsewhere (St Quirinus in Neuss, Roermond Minster).
In the 7th c. the hill with the Roman buildings became the seat of the Merovingian mayors of the palace, and in 689 Plectrude, wife of Pepin of Herstal, founded a religious house for noble ladies here, with a church which was rebuilt in the 10th c. The present church was built in the 11th c. by Abbess Ida, grand-daughter of the Emperor Otto II. The nave was consecrated by Pope Leo IX in 1049, the choir and crypt by Archbishop Anno in 1065. The importance of the church in the Middle Ages is measured by the fact that the Archbishop of Cologne celebrated the first of three Christmas midnight masses here. The severe damage suffered by the church during the last war has not yet been made good.

The west end has the monumentality characteristic of the west ends of Romanesque churches. The nave is dominated by the plain round-headed windows. The aisles are carried round the conches of the trilobate choir to form an ambulatory. The pilasters between the window sections show an alternation of red and white stone. The entrance for the congregation was formerly (and unusually) between the north and south conches.

The interior is 74 m/243 ft long and 52 m/171 ft wide between the north and south conches. An impressive feature of the west end is the upper storey (formerly the gallery occupied by the ladies of the convent), with its arcaded wall. In the nave the springing of the earlier vaulting which was not replaced during restoration can still be seen. Particularly striking is the centralising effect of the trilobate choir. The three-aisled crypt under the choir, with subsidiary rooms on either side, was modelled on the crypt of Speyer Cathedral; because of the fall of the ground towards the Rhine, its construction did not involve raising the floor of the choir.

Since the interior of the church is still in course of restoration the final positioning of the furnishings is not yet settled.
Of particular interest are the two 11th c. doors (at the entrance to the north conch) carved with scenes from the life of Christ; they begin on the left-hand door, at the top.
There are two fine grave slabs with figures of Plectrude. The older of the two (12th c.) shows her in the attitude of prayer, with her right hand raised; in the other (13th c.), which preserves remains of painting, she is holding in her left hand a model of the church (curiously, with a tower over the crossing). A small stone statue of a standing Madonna and Child (end of 12th c.) shows the severe forms of the Byzantine tradition. The seated Madonna of about 1200 appears rather coarsely carved: it was no doubt designed to be seen from some distance.
The richly painted "Limburg Madonna" (c. 1300), in a beautifully conceived pose, shows clear South German influence. Two figures of Christ as Saviour of the world and the Virgin as intercessor date from 1466. The fine forked cross of 1304 is one of a series of similar crosses, like those in St George's and St Severinus's.

Buses
132, 133

Trams
1, 2, 7

Opening times
During renovation only parts of church open

Exterior

Interior

Furnishings

85

St Mary´s in the Capitol

Details from St Mary´s . . .

. . . 11th century doors

The cloister to the west of the church is a 19th c. reconstruction. In the centre is a piece of sculpture by Marcks (1949), "The Mourners".
At Kasinostrasse 1–3 is the former Abbess's Lodging (1749). The Romantic writer Friedrich Schlegel lived in the house from 1804 to 1806.

Surroundings

On the east side of the church, between Marienplatz and Lichhof, stands the Three Kings Gate (Dreikönigenpförtchen), erected in 1330 on the spot where the relics of the Three Kings were brought into the town in 1164. The fine sculpture formerly on the gate, depicting the Adoration of the Kings, is now in the Schnütgen Museum (see entry).

Three Kings Gate

St Mary's in Kupfergasse (St Maria in der Kupfergasse)   M9 (L24)

In 1673–75 the Discalced (barefooted) Carmelite nuns, who had established themselves in Cologne in 1637 (see St Mary's of Peace), built a chapel to house the Black Virgin, and between 1705 and 1711 this was incorporated in a larger church.
The church is in the Baroque tradition of the Netherlands, which the nuns had brought with them from their mother house at's Hertogenbosch. The richly decorated Baroque interior was destroyed during the last war. After the war the Altar of the Maccabees (1717) was set up in the restored church. The statue of the Black Virgin is in the old chapel, at the north end of the nave.
The image of the Virgin plays an important part in popular piety. It is believed that the statue became black because it was carried through the streets of Cologne during an outbreak of plague in order to drive out the epidemic.

Location
Neven-DuMont-Strasse 7

U-Bahn
Appellhofplatz

Trams
3, 4, 5, 9, 11, 12, 16

Opening times
Throughout the day

---

*St Mary's in Lyskirchen (St Maria in Lyskirchen)   N10 (N26)

This little church is celebrated for its Romanesque frescoes, which are among the finest of their kind. The existence of an earlier church on the site is attested in 948, and in the 11th c. this was the private church of a landowner named Lysolphus (hence the name Lyskirchen) in the outlying district of Noithusen, which was brought within the walls of Cologne in the town's second extension of its boundaries in 1106. The present church dates from 1210–20, with 17th c. additions. Of all the churches in the city's central area this was the one that suffered least damage during the last war.
The main front faces on to the Rhine. The church gains its characteristic skyline from the north tower; the south tower was never completed. The interior is galleried. The two lowest stages of the tower form open halls in the choir.

Location
An Lyskirchen 8

Buses
132, 133

Trams
1, 2, 7

Opening times
Throughout the day

The 13th c. frescoes on the vaulting were discovered only in 1879. The cycle of greatest liturgical importance is the series of paintings in the central aisle. These, running from east to west, depict twelve New Testament scenes on the south side and twelve Old Testament scenes on the north side. The conception behind them is the prefiguration in the Old Testament of events which came to pass in the New Testament. Thus the promise

Frescoes

and the birth of Isaac (the sacrificial lamb of the Old Testament) have their counterpart in the promise and the birth of Christ (the sacrificial lamb of the New Testament). This conception is given specific expression in the half-length figures in the centre of the east vaulting: on the north side Lex, the Law of the Old Testament, and on the south side Gratia, the Grace of the New Testament.

Much better preserved than these paintings are the frescoes on the life of St Nicholas in the south vaulting of the tower. The life of St Catherine in the north vaulting of the tower shows 19th c. overpainting. Above the doorway in the west wall of the central aisle is a representation of the Adoration of the Kings. There is no doubt that paintings of this kind, to be seen in many medieval churches, were designed to serve as a kind of picture Bible for the unlearned who could neither read nor write.

Furnishings

At the west end of the south aisle is a 13th c. font with a 17th c. cover. Above the altar, in a modern mandorla, is a beautiful 14th c. Madonna of the Cologne school.

At the east end of the north aisle the "Boatmen's Madonna" (1420) recalls the old fishermen's settlement outside Cologne whose church this was.

St Mary's of Peace (St Maria vom Frieden)   N9

Location
Vor den Siebenburgen 6–10

In 1637 ten Carmelite nuns settled here, fleeing from the wars of religion in the Netherlands, and began to build a church,

St Mary's in Lyskirchen: St Nicholas

which owing to financial difficulties was not completed until 1716. Its most notable feature is the west front, in Netherlands Baroque style. The French Queen Marie de Médicis, driven out of France by Richelieu, presented to the nuns in 1642 the image of Our Lady of Peace (original lost; the one in the church is a 17th c. replacement). The convent was dissolved when all religious houses were secularised in 1803, and the church served as a parish church until it reverted to the Carmelites in 1949.

In the crypt (normally not open to visitors) is a memorial to Edith Stein, an assistant to the philosopher Edmund Husserl who became a convert to Catholicism in 1922, entered the Carmelite order and acquired considerable reputation for her writings, particularly on Thomas Aquinas. She was murdered in Auschwitz in 1942.

Trams
6, 15, 16

Opening times
Throughout the day

St Nicholas's Church (St Nikolaus)

See Brauweiler Abbey

**St Pantaleon's Church   N8/9 (O24)

St Pantaleon's, one of Cologne's oldest surviving churches, is of great interest in the history of architecture, particularly on account of its rood screen.

The first church on the site, built in 866, was enlarged by Archbishop Bruno in 957 after a Benedictine community was established here. In 984 Theophano, the Emperor Otto II's Greek wife, added the fine west end and the choir apse, and to her also was due the dedication of the church, unusual in the Roman Catholic West, to St Pantaleon, a saint popular in the Greek Orthodox church. Further extensions to the nave in 1152 gave the church its present basilican form. Most of the Late Gothic and Baroque alterations were swept away during the postwar rebuilding of the church.

Location
Am Pantaleonsberg 6

Trams
6, 10, 11, 12, 15, 16

The approach to the church is still through the old monastery wall, which marked out the area of sanctuary. The church is surrounded by buildings reflecting the original layout of the monastery.

St Pantaleon's is unique among the churches of Cologne in allowing us to appreciate the original character of one of the religious houses established just outside the old Roman walls (see entry). During the Middle Ages monasteries such as St Pantaleon's became the nucleus of settlements which were then enclosed within the Romanesque town walls (see entry) of 1180 and incorporated in the city (see Severinsviertel). The massive and imposing form of the west work, with its square tower rising above the projecting porch, flanked by the higher staircase towers, is probably to be explained by the fact that this was the Emperor's residence when he visited the monastery. The severe forms of the nave are somewhat relieved by the post-Gothic windows in the aisles.

Exterior

The interior, like the exterior, is dominated by the massive west tower. The use of purple-coloured stone in the arcading of the

Interior

St Pantaleon's Church

St Pantaleon's

Rood screen from south aisle

St Pantaleon's: the nave

double tier of chapels surrounding the 18 m/60 ft high space under the tower also points to the existence of an imperial residence in the west gallery. The nave recovered its original basilican character with the provision of a coffered ceiling in the postwar restoration. The east end of the church is notable particularly for the Late Gothic rood screen (*c*. 1500), with the Virgin in the centre, flanked by St Pantaleon on the right and St Maurice on the left, and beyond these St Quirinus and St John the Evangelist. Below the Virgin is St Veronica with the vernicle (the cloth with which she wiped Christ's face). On the gallery of the rood screen is an imposing organ of 1652.

In the south choir (St Paul's) can be seen the modern tomb of the Empress Theophano. On the west wall are 15th c. figures of knights, on the south wall paintings (12th–13th c.) from all over the church, on the east wall a 16th c. winged altar. The windows in the apse contain stained glass by H. Bruyn the Younger (1622). In the north choir (St Peter's) is the entrance to the crypt, with the Roman sarcophagus which contains the remains of Archbishop Bruno.

Furnishings

St Peter's Church

M9 (N24)

St Peter's is, apart from St Cecilia's, the only surviving example in Cologne of a "family" of churches – the juxtaposition of a collegiate and a parish church.

The church was originally built, perhaps in the late Roman period, on the site of Roman public baths. In the mid 12th c., when St Peter's became a parish church, a Romanesque basilican church was built, the west tower of which still survives. The present nave with its gallery was built in the early 16th c., financed by donations from wealthy Cologne families. During restoration after the last war the vaulted roof, which could not safely be rebuilt, was replaced by a coffered wooden ceiling.

Externally plain, the church has a fine interior. As the parish church of the second largest ward in Cologne, it has additional room for worshippers in its large galleries, which leave only the east wall and the apse free. The Late Gothic reticulated vaulting and windows (old stained glass in the lower sections, modern in the upper) contribute to the unity of the general effect.

In the Chapel of the Cross in the north porch can be seen the church's greatest treasure, Rubens's "Crucifixion of St Peter", one of his last paintings, commissioned in 1637 by the wealthy Jabach family. As a child Rubens had lived for almost ten years in nearby Sternengasse (No. 19).

Also in the Chapel of the Cross are a "Scourging of Christ" (15th c.) from South Tirol (northern Italy) and a Baroque figure of St Francis, rapt in ecstasy.

On the second pier in the nave (south side) is a Baroque figure of Joseph with the Infant Christ. The painting in the vaulting of the south aisle is Expressionist (early 20th c.).

On the second pier on the north side is a 15th c. Madonna in the style of the Rhineland.

On the wall of the apse, to the right, are the side panels of an altar of 1525.

The baptistery under the tower contains a bronze 16th c. font. Adjoining, to the left, is a Baroque "Annunciation".

Location
Leonard-Tietz-Strasse 6

U-Bahn
Neumarkt

Buses
136, 146

Trams
1, 2, 3, 4, 7, 9, 11, 12, 16

St Severinus's Church (St Severin) O9

Location
Severinskirchplatz

Buses
132, 133

Opening times
Closed at lunchtime

Two thousand years of history are impressively documented in St Severinus's and in the excavations underneath the church. The first church on this site was built about A.D. 320, perhaps by the first bishop of Cologne of whom we have record, Maternus, in the Roman cemetery flanking the road to the legionary camp at Bonn (on the line of present-day Severinstrasse: see Severinsviertel). The church was enlarged at the end of the 4th c. by Bishop Severinus, who was buried in the porch of his church. In the 8th c. a *confessio*, predecessor of the present crypt, seems to have been constructed in his honour. After various alterations and extensions Archbishop Bruno I conse-crated (948) a basilican church, the basis of the present 13th c. nave (altered in the Late Gothic period). The long choir and crypt were built in the 11th c.; the west tower was completed in 1411. The restoration of the church after wartime destruction was finished by 1950, but extensive further work was required in the late 1960s to maintain the stability of the structure.

Exterior

The tall west tower is in the Gothic style of the Lower Rhineland, very different from that of the Cathedral (see entry). The most notable feature of the nave is the Late Gothic windows; the apse is still in the Romanesque of the Hohenstaufen period.

Interior

The nave, basically Romanesque in conception, is given a distinctly Gothic accent by the large west window and the Gothic reticulated vaulting. The choir, raised to accommodate the crypt, is firmly Romanesque, with an articulation of the wall at the east end of the choir similar to that of other Cologne churches of the Hohenstaufen period (see St Gereon's).
During restoration work remains of Romanesque painting (a Crucifixion) were found in the vaulting of the choir.

Furnishings

The stained glass at the west end of the south aisle dates from about 1508 and was probably the work of the Master of St Severinus; it represents Christ on Calvary. Set into the wall of the aisle are a number of epitaphs. On the upper part of the wall is a small 17th c. triptych (Crucifixion, with donors). Farther east is the entrance to the former sacristy, now the Lady Chapel, with a Pietà of 1410 from Bamberg. On the east side of the pier at the entrance a tablet commemorates the sociologist B. Schmittmann, murdered by the Nazis in 1939.
At the west end of the south and north aisles can be seen a superb series of paintings on the legend of St Severinus (*c.* 1500) by the Master of St Severinus. On the west wall is a 14th c. plague cross.
The choir-stalls are the oldest in Cologne, dating from the 13th c. On the south wall of the choir is the twelve-year-old Jesus in the Temple (*c.* 1600), on the north wall a Crucifixion (18th c.). The two circular wall paintings farther east are 19th c. versions of 14th c. originals.
Behind the altar is the reliquary of St Severinus, an early 19th c. replacement of the valuable 11th c. original which was melted down in 1795. A circular enamel panel from the original reliquary depicting St Severinus is preserved in the Diocesan Museum (see entry).
At the east end of the north aisle is the entrance to the crypt and

the excavations (shown only on conducted tours: see below). On the last pier in the nave (NW corner) is the beautiful "Smiling Madonna" (*c.* 1280). Half way along the wall of the aisle is the entrance (usually closed) to the cloister. Set into the wall on either side of the doorway are a number of epitaphs. At the west end of the aisle can be found a late 15th c. triptych from the Netherlands, a fine Crucifixion with the donor (clad in white) kneeling below.

On the west wall, beside the entrance, is a 16th c. alabaster relief of the Last Supper and the Washing of the Feet.

The excavations and the crypt can be seen only on conducted tours (Monday and Friday at 4.30 p.m.).

Excavations and crypt

The excavations give an excellent impression of the large

Basilica of St Severinus

(former collegiate church)

4th c.

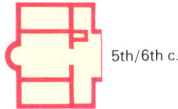
5th/6th c.

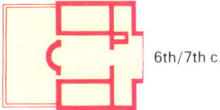
6th/7th c.

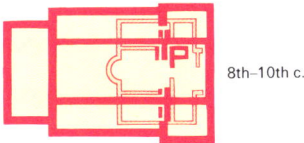
8th–10th c.

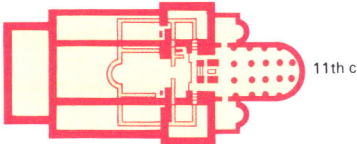
11th c.

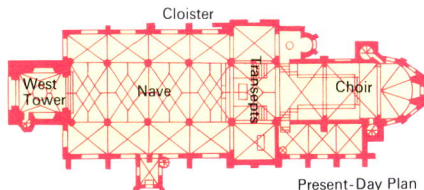

Cloister

West Tower | Nave | Transepts | Choir

Present-Day Plan

Stages of Development

FIRST BUILDING PERIOD
Building of a Cemetery Chapel (Zömeterial Church in 4th c.).

SECOND BUILDING PERIOD
Enlargement of original building by addition of two aisles and a triple east narthex (tomb of Bishop Severinus?) in 5th/6th c.

THIRD BUILDING PERIOD
In 6th/7th c. the church gets an outer courtyard surrounded by a wall.

FOURTH BUILDING PERIOD
At the turn of the 8th to 9th c. a new basilica arises almost twice the size of old one. This is the actual canonical church dedicated to St Severinus.

FIFTH BUILDING PERIOD
About the middle of the 10th c. (Archbishop Bruno I) the church is considerably enlarged.

SIXTH BUILDING PERIOD
Rebuilding of the choir with a crypt and two lateral choir chapels (dedication by Archbishop Hermann II, 1036-1056)

SEVENTH BUILDING PERIOD
Between 1230 and 1237 the choir is rebuilt and the apse enlarged. At the end of the 13th c. an Early Gothic nave is erected which from 1479 to the beginning of the 16th c. is converted to the Late Gothic style. The mighty West Tower is built between 1393 and 1411. During the Baroque age the only changes were to the interior.

93

St Stephen's Church

Legend of St Severinus

Smiling Madonna

numbers of burials lining the old Roman road. They range from the earliest cremation burials (1st c. A.D.) by way of the inhumation burials in sarcophagi of the 2nd and 3rd c. to the burials of the Frankish period in caskets formed of stone slabs (e.g. the tomb of a singer, identified by the representation of a lyre). In this cemetery, which is believed to have become a Christian place of burial by the end of the 2nd c., the excavators found what were clearly the foundations of earlier buildings preceding the present church. Plans of the excavation site, showing the periods to which the various remains belong, help visitors to understand the complexities of the site, with sarcophagi and walls packed close together and on top of one another.

The main crypt, under the choir, has remains of 13th c. wall paintings on the pentagonal east end (Romanesque of the Hohenstaufen period). In the north crypt, at the entrance, is a font of 1500.

St Stephen's Church (St Stephan)   O5/6

Location
Suitbert-Heimbach-Platz

Bus
146

This pretty little church, originally founded in Carolingian times, shows a mingling of many different architectural periods. The present nave was built about 900, the rectangular choir at the end of the 10th c.; the apse and tower were built about 1100; in the 13th c. an aisle was added on the north side and a court room (destroyed) on the south side; the sacristy dates only from the 18th c. St Stephen's has been in use as a parish church from at least 1224. It has a 12th c. font.

*St Ursula's Church   L9 (K25)

St Ursula's Church and the history of its construction, closely
bound up with the legend of St Ursula, are a striking illustration
of the importance (and the profitability) of the cult of relics in
the Middle Ages.
The origin of the church, as a surviving inscription records and
archaeological investigation has confirmed, goes back to a
memorial building erected in the 4th c. to commemorate a
number of female Christian martyrs. The earliest evidence of the
cult of these martyrs, however, dates only from the 9th c., and
the well known legend of St Ursula and her companions – the
story of the king's daughter and her companions who were
killed by the Huns besieging Cologne because Ursula refused
to become the wife of the leader of the Huns – is first referred
to in the 10th c. The discovery of numerous burials (in a Roman
cemetery flanking the road to Neuss) during the extension of
Cologne's boundaries in 1106 gave a powerful impetus to the
cult of relics and the trade in relics (which reached as far afield
as Finland, Portugal and Venice). The bones of dead Romans
became the remains of Ursula's 11,000 attendant virgins
(commemorated by the eleven tongues in Cologne's coat of
arms), and at the beginning of the 12th c. the present church,
a galleried basilica, was built as visible testimony to the very
considerable importance the cult had attained. The west tower
was built at the beginning of the 13th c., the Gothic choir and
Lady Chapel on the south side at its end. The Golden Chamber
and the Baroque culmination of the tower date from the 17th c.
– During the restoration of the church after the last war the
Gothic vaulting of the nave was replaced by a barrel roof.

The church is dominated by the severely Romanesque west
tower with its Baroque cap. The Romanesque nave contrasts
with the Gothic choir and south aisle.

The replacement of the Gothic vaulting (capitals of supporting
ribs preserved) by a timber roof has revealed the original
elevation of the walls of this galleried basilica, the first of its
kind in the Lower Rhineland. Galleries were later frequently
built in parish churches (e.g. St Mary's in Lyskirchen, St Peter's
– see entries), offering as they did more room for the
congregation. In St Ursula's, however, they were probably
required because of the numerous relics which attracted
pilgrims: the church belonged to a collegiate establishment of
only some ten or so noble ladies. – The Gothic choir, probably
built by the Cathedral workshops, is light and airy, with eleven
windows (19th and 20th c. stained glass) symbolising the
11,000 virgins.

The interior of the church is richly furnished. In the porch
(central pier on south side) is a 15th c. Pietà. Also housed
temporarily in the porch are some of the church's beautiful
choir-stalls, carved with scenes from the legend of St Ursula.
Notable features of the nave are the two-sided Late Gothic
reliquary busts on the nuns' gallery. On the front of the west
gallery is a 15th c. figure of Christ.
The Lady Chapel which opens off the south aisle formerly
contained a painting of the Virgin by the Master of the Life of
the Virgin, presented to the church in the 15th c. by Everhard

Location
Ursulaplatz 30

U-Bahn
Breslauer Platz

Trams
5, 9, 11, 12, 16

Opening times
Closed at lunchtime

Conducted tours
Church: Mon.–Thurs.
10–11 a.m.
Golden Chamber:
Sun. 11 a.m.–noon

Exterior

Interior

Furnishings

Detail from the legend of St Ursula

von Hirtz, which is now in the Alte Pinakothek in Munich. On the east wall is a statue of Christ and to the left of the entrance a figure of the Virgin (both 15th c.).

On the east wall of the south transept can be seen a fine series of portraits of the Apostles painted in oils on slabs of slate (13th c.). In a niche on the right, adjoining the choir, is a 14th c. forked cross; the figures of St John and the Virgin are 15th c. To the left of this a 16th c. alabaster relief portrays the Descent of the Holy Ghost. The 19th c. reliquary of St Ursula in the high choir preserves a few pieces of cloisonné enamel from the original 12th c. reliquary. In front of the reliquary is the Gothic high altar, with figures of 1890.

In the north transept, to the left, is a fine 15th c. statue of St Ursula, probably by Tilman van der Burch. On the west and east walls a superb cycle of paintings illustrates the legend of St Ursula (1456, school of Stephan Lochner). In the centre of the transept is the 17th c. tomb of St Ursula, with the 15th c. Gothic sarcophagus visible through openings in its sides. On the north side is a 17th c. oil painting of the (legendary) finding of St Ursula's tomb.

On the north-west pier of the crossing is a limestone Madonna of the 14th c.

Against the last pier in the nave before the porch is a child's sarcophagus of the Romanesque period, and above this a 16th c. limestone relief of the Bearing of the Cross.

Golden Chamber

The Golden Chamber (Goldene Kammer) was built in 1643 at the expense of a high imperial dignity named Johann von Crane and his wife to house the church's numerous relics and reliquaries. It gives a curious and rather macabre impression of medieval attitudes to the cult of relics, some of the large collection of bones having been used to form ornaments and symbols on the walls. On the east wall is an altar showing St Ursula in ecstasy (at top). Note particularly, in addition to the reliquary busts, more than a hundred in number, the reliquary of St Aetherius, St Ursula's legendary betrothed, in the centre of the room (*c.* 1170).

Further treasures, including precious fabrics and liturgical utensils, are preserved in the Treasury at the north-west corner of the church.

Treasury

Schauspielhaus (Theatre)

See Opera House and Theatre

Schnütgen Museum (St Cecilia's Church)   M9 (N24)

The Schnütgen Museum, now housed in St Cecilia's Church, is one of Germany's finest collections of medieval art. The collection was assembled by Alexander Schnütgen (1843–1918), a member of the Cathedral chapter from 1887, and presented by him to the city of Cologne in 1906; many of

Location
Cäcilienstrasse 29

U-Bahn
Neumarkt

Bust of the Parler school

Raising of Lazarus

Schnütgen Museum

Buses
136, 146

Trams
1, 2, 3, 4, 7, 9, 11, 12, 16

Opening times
Tues.–Sun. 10 a.m.–5 p.m.;
first Wed. in month
10 a.m.–8 p.m.

the objects were acquired on the secularisation of church property. St Cecilia's was first used to accommodate the collection in 1956; and after reconstruction of the interior of the church the museum, with additional material from the Wallraf-Richartz Museum (see entry), was reopened in 1977.

The exhibits are beautifully displayed and explained, and the "Polyvision" system, operated by pressing a button, displays comprehensive information on the exhibits themselves and on their history and significance. The various objects, of the highest artistic quality, form a harmonious unity with the Romanesque architecture of the church.

There are conducted tours on the first Wednesday in the month at 6.30 p.m. and on alternate Sundays at 11 a.m., or by arrangement.

The following is a selection of items of particular interest (arranged broadly according to period).

Museum Hall

On the north side is the "Commandments Window" from Boppard (1440–46): below St Elizabeth, above the Commandments. The windows on the west side, from Altenberg Abbey and St Apern's Church in Cologne, depict scenes from the life of St Bernard of Clairvaux; they date from the early 16th c.

North Gallery

Byzantine and early medieval art; fine ivories; book covers.

Nave

Magnificent Romanesque sculpture: e.g. Christ on the Cross with Mary and Joseph (11th c.), from St George's Church, and South Tirolese figures from Sonnenburg (early 13th c.). At the west end are two tympana from St Cecilia's Church and St Pantaleon's (both *c.* 1160, see entries) and the Siegburg Madonna (*c.* 1150).

North aisle

The north aisle is mainly devoted to Madonnas of the Early and High Gothic periods, most of them from the Cologne area or the Lower Rhineland. Another notable item (on one of the piers) is a fine bust of the Parler school, created around 1390 by a member of the family which developed at that period the new Gothic manner known as the "beautiful" or "soft" style.

Choir

Gothic items, including the Wasserberg choir-stalls (Lower Rhineland, *c.* 1300; on right, at near end, the donor kneeling before the Virgin), figures from the high altar of Cologne Cathedral and statues of the Three Kings (*c.* 1320) from the Three Kings Gate (see St Mary's in the Capitol).

Sacristy

The sacristy, on the north side of the choir, displays magnificent priestly vestments and fabrics.

South aisle

Late Gothic sculpture. Many figures show the characteristic sideways movement of the body, as in the Virgin by Tilman van der Burch (*c.* 1480) and St Nicodemus (Lower Rhineland, *c.* 1480). Lively narrative representations are St Jerome with the lion (*c.* 1460) and the raising of Lazarus (Westphalian, *c.* 1520).

Crypt

The (finely restored) crypt at the west end of the nave contains goldsmiths' work, mainly liturgical utensils.

South and West Galleries

The South Gallery contains small sculpture of the Late Gothic period, the West Gallery art of the Baroque period.

Schnütgen Museum
in the former Church of St Cecilia

St Cecilia's is one of the famous Romanesque Churches of Cologne (built 1130-1160). It was erected on the site of the Roman baths as the church of a home for ladies of the nobility (founded in 9th c.; from 1479 and Augustinian nunnery). Following its deconsecration in 1802 the church was at first used as a warehouse and later as a chapel for the civil hospital on the Neumarkt. After being considerably damaged in the Second World War St Cecilia's was restored from 1947 and in 1956 became the home of the **Schnütgen Museum**.

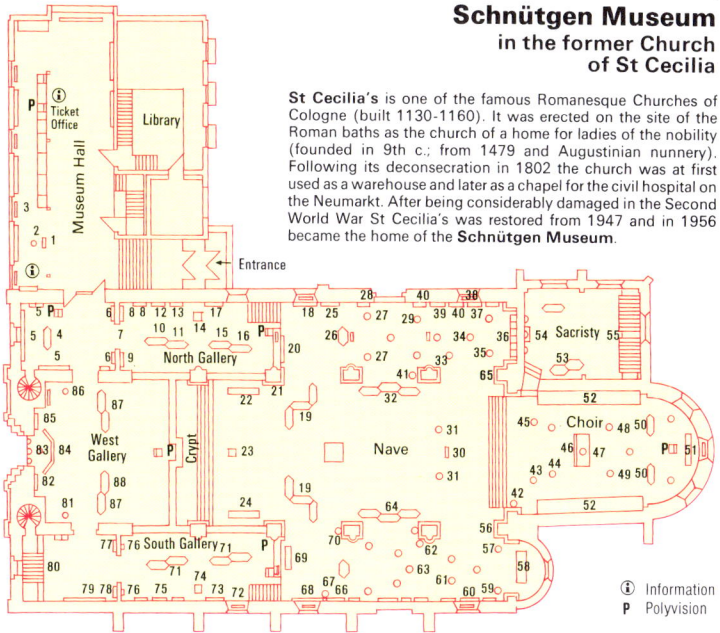

ⓘ Information
P Polyvision

MUSEUM HALL
1 Christ on the Ass
2 The Virgin Mary and Anna Selbdritt
3 Panel of St Bernard

BYZANTINE ART
4 Anno Chasuble
5 Textiles
6 Bronze Cast

CAROLINGIAN AND OTTONIAN ART
7 Scroll relief
8 Small works of art
9 Ivory, Byzantine panel, Death of the Virgin
10 Ivory book cover
11 Monstrance
12 Illumination
13 Limoges
14 St Heribert's comb
15 Crosses
16 Reliquary

ROMANESQUE ART
17 Birth star of the Virgin
18 Processional Crosses
19 Liturgical articles
20 Fiddler and dancer
21 Crucifix
22 Tympanum of St Pantaleon
23 Siegburg Madonna
24 Tympanum (St Cecilia)
25 Death of Mary
26 Wood sculpture
27 The Virgin
28 Angel of the Annunciation
29 Grieving Madonna
30 Crucifix of St George
31 Sonnenburg figures

GOTHIC
32 Small sculptures
33 Busts of Parler school
34 Friesentor Madonna
35 The Virgin
36 Busts of St Ursula, reliquary
37 Glass panels
38 St John and the founder
39 Choir of angels
40 Ivory
41 St Catherine
42 Apostles
43 The Virgin
44 Ollesheim Madonna
45 The Virgin enthroned
46 Altar veil from St Ursula's
47 Altar Cross
48 The Virgin enthroned
49 The Virgin from Kendenich
50 Figures from the Cathedral
51 Figures from the Three Kings Gateway
52 Wassenberg choir stalls
53 Sculptures
54 Triumphal Cross Group
55 Paraments

LATE GOTHIC
56 John the Baptist
57 Anna Selbdritt
58 Passion Altar
59 Noli me tangere
60 Hill of Calvary
61 St George
62 St Nicodemus
63 The Virgin Mary
64 Small sculptures
65 St Vigilius
66 St John's keys
67 St Bartholomew
68 Tabernacle
69 The Three Kings
70 St Hieronymus
71 Small sculpture
72 The Madonna in Glory
73 Domestic Altar
74 Rosary
75 Panels
76 Angel with banner

BAROQUE
77 Reliquary jars
78 Clay figures
79 Mass vestments of Maria Theresa
80 Paraments
81 The Madonna over the moon and a serpent
82 Model of an altar
83 View of the organ
84 Heisterbach grille
85 Ivory
86 St Joseph
87 Small sculpture
88 Memento mori

Severinstor (St Severinus Gate)

See Romanesque town walls

*Severinsviertel (St Severinus quarter)   N/O9 (N/O25)

Location
In and around Severinstrasse

Buses
132, 133

Trams
3, 4, 9

The Severinsviertel has preserved much of the character of old Cologne. It draws its particular atmosphere from a number of fine buildings containing notable works of art, an urbanity developed over many years and a well balanced population of natives and incomers, with a touch of the south thrown in.

In Roman times the dead were buried alongside the road to Bonn (which followed the line of present-day Severinstrasse), outside the town walls as the Twelve Tables of Roman law (5th c. B.C.) required. Excavations under St Severinus's Church (open to the public: see entry) have revealed remains of this cemetery area, together with a 4th c. Christian church. A considerable sensation was caused in 1967 by the excavation of the tomb of a wealthy Roman named Poblicius (now to be seen in the Roman-Germanic Museum, see entry) at Chlodwigplatz 24.

After the Roman period St Severinus's Church continued to grow. It already owned property in the 4th c., and by the 10th the religious house which is known to have existed at least as early as the 9th c. owned the whole area between the Roman walls (see entry) in the north, the line of Severinstrasse, Perlengraben and Schnurgasse in the west and their southward continuation (5 km/3 miles) to Höningen, and the Rhine in the east: a very large estate indeed. Other religious houses were established within this area, including St George's in the 11th c. Weavers also settled here and in the 11th c. the church of St John the Baptist became their parish church. Further development took place in 1180 with the construction of the Romanesque town walls (see entry). Within the enlarged city boundaries craftsmen and merchants settled along the old Roman road, combining with the settlements around monasteries to create sizeable built-up areas. The character of the area, however, was still predominantly rural. Street names such as "Im Ferkulum" recall former monastic landholdings – in this case a vineyard belonging to St Severinus's – from which the monks received a *ferculum* (contribution). The Bottmühle, a tower on the Romanesque town walls, is a reminder of the days when the mill was required to grind corn grown in the area. Of the monastic churches there still survive, in addition to St Severinus's and St George's, the Carthusian Church and St Mary's of Peace (see entries), but the farms which they owned have long since gone. An old brewhouse still survives at Severinstrasse 15, the 17th c. Balchem brewhouse (see Balchem House).

In 1802, during the French occupation, the religious houses were dissolved and their estates sold. During the 19th c. the fields disappeared, giving place to the factories and workers' dwellings of the industrial age. The Stollwerck chocolate factory was established in 1839, and a starch factory occupied

Market in front of St Severinus's Church ▶

the old Seyen convent (now destroyed: the name, distorted, is preserved in the form Sion: e.g. the Sion brewery).

After a period of general economic depression in the mid 19th c. a further upsurge in development made it necessary to pull down the old Romanesque town walls, and Cologne now started in earnest to expand beyond its limits of 1180. Outside the old circuit of walls there grew up the district of Neustadt ("New Town"), and much building of this period still survives between the Bonner Strasse and the Rhine. To this period belong, for example, the blocks of flats in the Severinsviertel with their handsome late 19th c. façades. In the course of the 20th c. the larger factories have tended to move to the outskirts of the city, leaving small craft industries and residential property.

The Second World War wrought devastation in the Severins-viertel, but in the postwar rebuilding the structure of the quarter was largely preserved, though the ramp leading up to the Severinsbrücke and the Ulrichgasse development have cut it in two. In recent years there has been much interest in plans to rehabilitate the district, preserving as much of it as possible. There are, however, many problems: many buildings are decayed beyond repair, and the population includes a high proportion of old people and 30 per cent of foreigners. Then, too, the Südstadt quarter has been "discovered" as a desirable residential area, with the inevitable consequences of rising rents and property speculation. There is also still controversy over the future use of the old Stollwerck chocolate factory.

It is very much to be hoped that bureaucratic organisation and speculation will not destroy an area which has grown up over many hundreds of years and – with all the minor imperfections which contribute to the character of the quarter – still preserves its fresh charm and urbanity.

Stadtgarten (Municipal Gardens) — L8

Location
Venloer Strasse/
Spichernstrasse

Trams
3, 4, 5, 6, 10, 15

The Stadtgarten, laid out in 1827–29, is Cologne's oldest public park; for there were no princely rulers here to lay out parks for purposes of show, and until the 19th c. planning of the Neustadt development (before which there was no town planning to speak of in Cologne) little provision was made for open spaces in the city. The Stadtgarten is laid out on the pattern of an English landscaped garden, with an abundance of handsome trees. At the north-west corner of the gardens is New St Alban's Church (see entry).

Synagogue — N8

Location
Roonstrasse 50

Trams
6, 10, 11, 12, 15, 16

The Synagogue (designed by Emil Schreiterer and Bernhard Below, 1895–99) is built on a centralised plan and roofed with a dome. Damage caused by the Nazis in 1938 and during the Second World War was made good in 1958–59.

Rathenauplatz, to the south-west of the Synagogue, was laid out in 1881, under the name Königsplatz, as part of the plan for the development of the Neustadt quarter. It was designed to be used for the marshalling of the Carnival processions. Now refashioned with gardens, it still preserves many handsome late 19th c. house fronts.

"Colonius", Telecommunications Tower

St George's Church, west end

*Telecommunications Tower ("Colonius")   L7

Cologne's Telecommunications Tower, known as "Colonius", is at present the fifth largest in the Federal Republic (243·3 m/ 798 ft high; 14·9 m/49 ft in diameter at the base, 8·8 m/29 ft at the platform). It was built to complete the Post Office's network of directional radio links. The platform, reached by lifts, has technical installations on the uppermost level; below this is a viewing platform with a cafeteria (at a height of 170 m/560 ft); and below this again is a restaurant (open in the evening as well as during the day) which revolves slowly on its axis.
In clear weather the view extends to the Siebengebirge in the south and Düsseldorf in the north. The view of Cologne itself is particularly fine: the growth of the city in concentric rings is clearly recognisable in the street pattern.

Location
Innere Kanalstrasse
(near Venloer Strasse)

Trams
3, 4, 5

Theatre (Schauspielhaus)

See Opera House and Theatre

**Town Hall (Rathaus)   M9 (M25)

Cologne's Town Hall has grown in size down the centuries through successive extensions and enlargements. This centre

Location
Rathausplatz

103

Town Hall

Buses
132, 133

Opening times
Mon.–Fri. 8 a.m.–5 p.m.,
Sat. 10 a.m.–4 p.m.
(Hanseatic Hall and Rent
Chamber only on conducted
tours)

Conducted tours
Mon., Wed. and Sat. at 3 p.m.

of civic administration still occupies the same site as did the administration in Roman times (see Praetorium).

A first Burghers' House erected in 1130 in what was then the Jewish quarter (as the name of the Judengasse still bears witness) was replaced in 1360 by the Hanseatic Hall (Hansasaal). The tower was built by the town's guilds in 1407–14 as a symbol of their victory over the patricians. The Lion Court (Löwenhof) dates from 1540, the Loggia from 1569–73. In 1548 and subsequent years the Town Hall was enlarged by taking in other buildings on the east side, towards the Old Market, and the 17th c. saw the erection of the Spanish Building (Spanischer Bau: named after the Spanish League, which entered into a military alliance here in 1623). After the last war the tower, the loggia and the Hanseatic Hall were re-erected. The whole of the complex on the Old Market and south sides and the Spanish Building (under which remains of the Roman Praetorium were found) were replaced by new building. Since part of the Town Hall occupies the site of the Roman river harbour, now filled in (see Rheinvorstadt), it was necessary, in order to ensure the stability of the building, to insert 91 reinforced concrete piers.

Exterior

The new east front facing the Old Market has been the subject of controversy, since it spoils the unity of the square. The 61 m/ 200 ft high tower at the north end has the air of a castle keep but also reflects the architectural style of Gothic churches. The deliberate use of architectural types which had been developed by the nobility and the church as a demonstration of their status and authority indicates the independent spirit of the guilds, the new masters of the city.

One feature restored after the war was "Platz Jabbeck" (below the clock on the east side), a grotesque figure (15th c.) which sticks its tongue out every time the hour is struck: a rough and vigorous way (cf. the "Kallendresser", see Rheinvorstadt) of telling the old rulers of the city what time it was. Many of the figures on the façade of the tower are still missing, but there are many interesting and piquant details, particularly on the north side, to be made out with the aid of binoculars.

On the west side, at the north-west corner of Rathausplatz, is the new Spanish Building. In an excavation at the south-west corner remains of the Aula Regia, which formed part of the Roman Praetorium (see entry), can be seen. To the west of this were the synagogue and mikvah (ritual bath: open Sun. 11 a.m.–1 p.m., Mon.–Thurs. 8 a.m.–5 p.m., Fri. 8 a.m.–noon; key from car park attendant). The Jews were settled in this area from the 10th c.; they were expelled in 1424.

After the destruction of the synagogue the Town Hall chapel (itself destroyed during the last war) was built in its place (1426). In this chapel was Stephan Lochner's painting of the city's patron saints (1445: now in the Cathedral, see entry), showing the independent burghers of Cologne as directly represented in the courts of heaven by their patrons, without mediation by the churchmen or nobles who were normally present in such scenes.

Loggia (Laube)

On the east side of the Town Hall is the renaissance loggia, from the upper floor of which the resolutions of the municipal council were announced. On the balustrade can be seen a representation of Burgomaster Gryn's victorious struggle with

Town Hall: the tower and loggia ▶

Town Hall

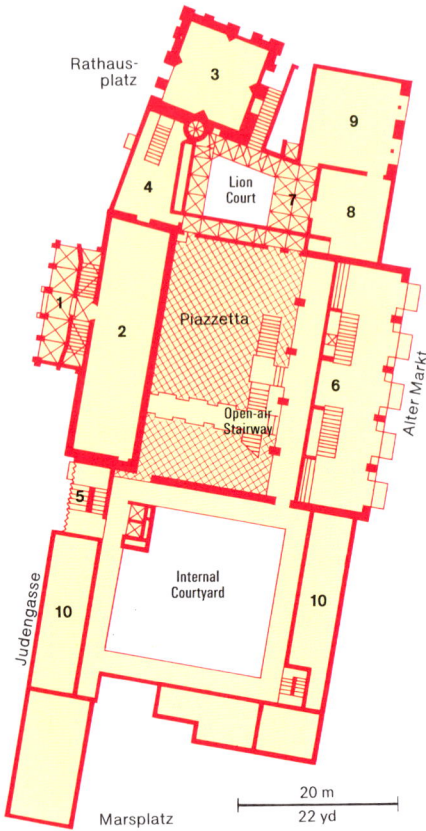

1 Renaissance Loggia
(originally of 1573)
2 Hall Building
   Ground Floor: Entrance Hall
    (Bronze Door by H.
    Gernot)
   Upper Floor: Hansa Room
    (originally the 'Long
    Room'; Gothic tracery
    rosettes; wooden
    figures "Eight
    Prophets", originally
    c. 1410; stone figures
    "Nine Worthies",
    originally c. 1360)
3 Tower
   Basement: Tower Cellar
   Ground Floor: Bursary
   First Floor: Senate Chamber
    Ceremonial Doorway and
    Councillors' Seating;
    intarsia work by
    Melchior von Reidt,
    1601)
4 Prophets' Chamber
(wooden doorway from the Arsenal;
intarsia work by Melchior von Reidt,
1600)
5 Bronze Wall
Bronze elements and plexiglass bars as
panelling for the stairwell
6 Main Building
   Ground Floor: Information hall
    Plasmann Cellar
   First Floor: Offices of the Mayor
   Second Floor: Offices of the Chief
    Executive
7 Lion Court Ambulatory
(on first floor; St Peter's Well, alabaster
work of 1662)
8 White Hall (on first floor; modern
tapestry by F. Ahrend)
9 Shell Room (on first floor; modern
tapestry by J. Faßbender)
10 Offices

the lion into whose den the cathedral authorities had thrown him: an allusion to the burghers' successful struggle for independence. Round the lower cornice of the loggia are portrait heads of Roman emperors.

Interior

The new entrance hall gives access to the Piazzetta, a small covered court with portraits of burgomasters of Cologne on its walls. To the north of this is the ambulatory round the Renaissance Lion Court (Löwenhof). On the west side of this is "St Peter's Well" (Petrusbrunnen), the remains of an alabaster Lady Altar (1662) which formerly stood in the Cathedral. On the ground floor of the tower, to the north of the Lion Court, is the Rent Chamber (Rentkammer), now used for marriages. This was originally the seat of the city's financial administration, which on particular days in the year made payments (*renten*, rents) here.

"Platz Jabbeck"

One of the Nine Worthies

On the upper floor of the Town Hall, above the entrance hall, is the Hanseatic Hall (Hansasaal), given this name in the 19th c. in honour of the Hanse, the association of merchants which met here in 1367 and resolved on war with King Valdemar Atterdag of Denmark. On the north wall are a Gothic rose window (restored) and figures of the eight Prophets. On the south wall are the Nine Worthies of pagan, Jewish and Christian times (14th c.). Above them is the Emperor Charles IV, who granted Cologne the right of staple (see Rheinvorstadt, Stapelhaus) in 1349 and the right of fortification in 1335; the figure of the Emperor is flanked by personifications of these rights.

Hanseatic Hall

Trade Fair Grounds (Messegelände) and Rheinpark

K18–M 10/11 (K/L27)

Cologne's long tradition as a city of far-flung trading connections and busy fairs has been maintained in the 20th c. In 1914 the Werkbund (Craft Union) Exhibition was held on this site in Deutz, and in 1922, on the initiative of Senior Burgomaster Konrad Adenauer, a trade fair complex (designed by Verbeek and Pieper) was established here. It was enlarged by Abel in 1927 on the occasion of the Press Exhibition. The whole complex, built in brick, is precisely articulated. From the tower (restaurant, reached by lift; fine view) Oskar Kokoschka painted his "View of Cologne" (1956: now in the Wallraf-Richartz Museum – see entry).

Location
Deutz

Trams
1, 2, 3, 4

To the north, on the banks of the Rhine, is the Dancing Fountain (Tanzbrunnen) of 1950, where concerts and dance shows are given in summer, and beyond this the Rheinpark, where the German Federal Garden Show was held in 1957 and 1971, with flowerbeds, ponds, hothouses, a narrow-gauge railway and a spa establishment. It is linked by a cableway alongside the Zoobrücke (Zoo Bridge) with the other bank of the Rhine.

Trinity Church (St Trinitatis)   N9 (N26)

Location
Filzengraben 6

Buses
132, 133

Trams
1, 2, 7

It was not until 1797, during the French occupation, that Protestants were admitted to the rights of citizenship in Cologne, and in 1802 they were granted freedom of worship. The Antonite Church then became their first parish church.
The Trinity Church, the first church erected in Cologne by Protestants, was built in 1857–60 – interestingly enough, in the area of the old merchant town (see Martinsviertel and Overstolz House) – and became the parish church of the city's Protestant merchants. It was designed by August Stüler, a pupil of Karl Friedrich Schinkel, in the style of an early Christian basilica, mainly in order to distinguish it from the Roman Catholic churches of Cologne, which were Romanesque or Gothic. It is a good example of late neo-classical architecture of the Berlin school, with its vaulted porch, surmounted by a rose window, and the predominantly round arches of the interior.

Ubii, Monument of the

See Roman walls

Ursuline Church (Corpus Christi)   L9 (K26)

Location
Machabäerstrasse 75

Trams
5, 9, 11, 12, 16

After being driven out of Liège during the Thirty Years War a community of Ursulines settled in the neutral city of Cologne in 1639. In 1651 they were granted permission to stay, and thereupon founded the first secondary school for girls in Germany. In 1709 the Venetian Matteo Alberti, court architect to Elector Johann Wilhelm, patron of the Ursuline order, was commissioned to build the church. Clearly in the tradition of the Baroque churches of northern Italy, it is a good example of the influence of court architecture in a city ruled by its burghers.

Volksgarten (People's Gardens)   O8/9

Location
Volksgartenstrasse

Tram
12

The Volksgarten was laid out in 1887–89 as part of the plan for the development of the Neustadt area. It incorporates a fort belonging to the town's Prussian fortifications, now a rose-garden. On the little lake is a beer-garden.
The houses round the gardens, particularly in Volksgartenstrasse and Vorgebirgsstrasse on the east side, have well preserved façades of the late 19th c. period of rapid industrial development.

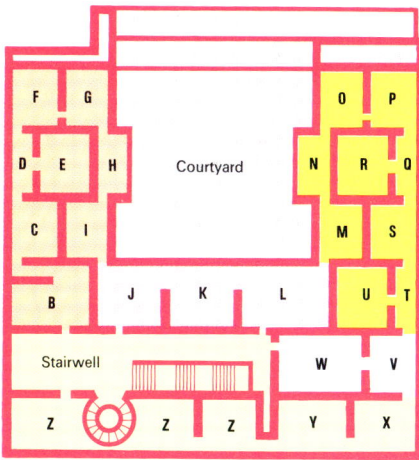

Wallraf-Richartz Museum and Ludwig Museum

N↓

The **Wallraf-Richartz Museum** (art from 1300-1900, and the **Ludwig Museum** (20th c. art) are now housed, together with the Philharmonia, in a new terraced cultural complex between the Cathedral and the Rhine. The two museums were formerly in the building "An der Recht-schule" which now houses part of the Museums of Applied Art. The new complex was opened on September 6. 1986.

Wallraf-Richartz Museum

☐ Painting of the Middle Ages

☐ Painting of the 16th c.

☐ Flemish and Dutch Painting

☐ Paintings from Romanesque Countries

☐ Painting of the 19th c.

Ludwig Museum: Modern Gallery
International art of the 20th c.

**Wallraf-Richartz Museum and Ludwig Museum   M9 (L25)

The Wallraf-Richartz Museum contains a collection of painting down to 1900, with special emphasis on the Middle Ages, particularly the Cologne school of painters. The Ludwig Museum has an excellent collection (with some gaps) of 20th c. painting down to the present day; its display of Pop Art in particular is internationally renowned. Shortage of space means that both museums can show only a selection from their extensive holdings, and from time to time there are exhibitions of items from their reserves.

The nucleus of the Wallraf-Richartz Museum was assembled by Ferdinand Franz Wallraf, a priest who became Rector of the University, by purchases from the church property secularised in 1802, and bequeathed by him to the city of Cologne in 1824. A wealthy merchant named Johann Heinrich Richartz donated money in 1851 for the construction of a museum to house the steadily increasing collection.

This first museum, built on the site of a Minorite convent, did not survive the Second World War. The Wallraf-Richartz collection, much increased by later donations and purchases, is now housed on the first floor of the new building (1955–56) on the same site; from the inner courtyard there is a fine view of the cloister side of the Minorite church. The rooms, from B to Z, are arranged in chronological order.

Location
Rheinufer

U-Bahn
Dom/Hauptbahnhof

Buses
132, 133

Trams
5, 9, 11, 12, 16

Opening times
Wed. and Fri.–Sun. 10 a.m.– 5 p.m., Tues. and Thurs. 10 a.m.–8 p.m.; particular departments closed at varying times

Conducted tours
Sat. and Sun. at 11 a.m., Tues. at 6 p.m., and by arrangement (tel. 2 21 23 78)

Wallraf-Richartz Museum

Rooms B–J	Rooms B–J are devoted to medieval painting, with particular emphasis on the Cologne school. Room B: early examples of international Gothic (including the Wehrden Crucifixion, c. 1340. Room C: works by Stephan Lochner, the leading representative of the Cologne school (Madonna in the Rose-Garden, c. 1445). Room E: St Anne with the Virgin and the Infant Jesus, by the Master of the Glorification of the Virgin, c. 1480; in the background a view of Cologne. Room F: works by the Master of the Life of the Virgin. Room G: Altar of the Holy Kinship, by the Master of the Holy Kinship (after 1500). Room J: "St Ursula with her Parents" by the Master of St Severinus, in the medieval tradition, and "Portrait of a Woman" by the same artist, reflecting the new conceptions of the Renaissance (both after 1500); Hans Memling's "Nativity".
Room K	Renaissance painting (B. Bruyn's double portrait of the Salsburgs, husband and wife).
Room L	Dürer's "Drummer and Piper", Hieronymus Bosch's "Nativity", works by Baldung Grien, Cranach, etc.
Rooms M–U	Flemish and Dutch painting: still life by Snyders in Room P; Rubens and van Dyck in Rooms Q and R; Ruysdael, Jan van de Kappelle and Frans Hals in Room S; Rembrandt, including the fine "Self-Portrait in Old Age", in Room U.
Rooms V and W	French, Spanish and Italian painting. Room V: Canaletto, Tiepolo, Claude Lorrain, Boucher. Room W: Claude Lorrain, Murillo, Ribera.
Rooms X–Z	19th c. painting: C. D. Friedrich, Rottmann, Menzel; Stuck, Böcklin, Leibl, Klinger; Feuerbach, Slevogt, Uhde, Liebermann; Courbet, Corot, Pissarro, Renoir; Cézanne, van Gogh, Monet, Gauguin, Edvard Munch.
Staircase hall	Pictures by Corinth, etc.

Ludwig Museum

Cologne owes the preservation of much modern art to a lawyer named Josef Haubrich, who saved many works, particularly by exponents of Expressionism and Verism, during the Nazi period. The Ludwig Museum was founded in 1976, when the Aachen industrialist Peter Ludwig presented much of his collection to the city on condition that a special building was erected for the new museum. The new building opened in 1986, to the east of the Cathedral, was designed to house the Wallraf-Richartz Museum as well. It has been the subject of much controversy, both on grounds of cost and as an intrusion into this part of the old town. On the positive side, however, it must be said that the Ludwig Museum has given Cologne a collection of modern art which in certain fields is of outstanding importance.

The main part of Haubrich's collection is on the second floor.

Vincent van Gogh: Bridge

S. Lochner: Madonna in the Rose-Garden

Marc Chagall: Moses

Room 22 contains Expressionists: members of the "Brücke" group like Kirchner, Heckel and Schmidt-Rottluff; Modigliani, Vlaminck, Matisse; Chagall, Jawlensky, Nolde.
Rooms 1–3 follow on with Verism and Neue Sachlichkeit (Functional Art): Beckmann, Grosz, Dix, Radziwill; Kokoschka, Lehmbruck; Hoerle, Räderscheidt, Seiwert.
Room 4: Klee; Marc, Macke, Feininger.
Rooms 5–9 are devoted to Surrealism, Informal Art, Forensic Art and Nouveau Réalisme: Ernst, Dali, Magritte, de Chirico; Miró, Baumeister, Cornell, Giacometti, Bacon; Dubuffet, Oelze, Tapiés, Klein, Fontana.

Picasso

Room 21 is devoted to Picasso, with works ranging from his Cubist period to his last phase.

Abstract painting

Rooms 21–14 (in chronological order) display abstract painting, from Room 19 (Cubism) by way of Rooms 18 and 17 (an excellent representation of Russian painting of the Constructivist and Suprematist schools, including particularly Malewitsch) to the international abstract painting of the Bauhaus and De Stijl (Moholy-Nagy, Mondrian), Vasarely and the Abstract Expressionism of the Americans (Pollock, Newman, Kline, Rothko).

Pop Art

Rooms 13–10 contain an outstanding collection of Pop Art: Oldenburg, Rauschenberg, Dine, Warhol, Segal, Johns, Rosenquist, Lichtenstein, Indiana, Wesselmann, Hamilton.

Staircase hall

In staircase hall on 2nd floor: Beuys, Twombly, Matisse, Richter, Noland, Soulanges. On stair to 1st floor: Jorn, Appel, Mathieu, Tobey, Saint Phalle. Stair to ground floor: Johns, Indiana, Lichtenstein.

Ground floor

Duane Hanson, E. Kienholz, Warhol, Noland, Stella, Baselitz, Tinguely.

Graphic art and photography

Only selections of the museum's holdings of graphic art and photography can be displayed. The reserve collections can be seen by appointment.
The reference library on the ground floor is open to the public.

Weckschnapp

See Romanesque town walls

* *Zons

Distance
30 km/19 miles N

Access
Train to Dormagen, then bus

Zons is a picturesque little town particularly notable for its medieval walls, the best preserved in the Rhineland. It is now part of Dormagen.
Central to the history of Zons was the decision by the Archbishop of Cologne, Friedrich (III) von Saarwerden, to transfer the customs post on the Rhine from Neuss to Zons, which then lay directly on the river (1372). Hitherto merely a grange belonging to the archbishopric (attested from the 11th c.), it now became a fortified town. The importance of the

Manorhouse and Juddeturm, Zons

customs dues was very considerable, accounting as they did for more than half the annual revenue of the Archbishops and Electors. All goods transported on the Rhine which passed through the Zons customs post paid dues of between 2 per cent and 10 per cent of their value, the amount being reckoned in tuns of wine (the most important merchandise transported on the Rhine).

Zons passed into the hands of the chapter of Cologne Cathedral in 1463, when Archbishop Dietrich von Moers pledged the Zons customs dues to the citizens of Cologne. A struggle for possession of Zons between Archbishop Ruprecht von der Pfalz, seeking to recover the archbishopric together with the profitable towns of Neuss and Zons, and Cologne developed into a war affecting the whole Empire, with Charles the Bold of Burgundy supporting Ruprecht and the Emperor Frederick III coming in on the side of Cologne. The conflict ended in 1475 with the defeat of Charles the Bold, and Zons remained in the hands of Cologne.

The period between the end of the 16th and the end of the 18th c. was a time of decline for Zons, as a result of various wars (including the Thirty Years War) and changes in the course of the Rhine taking it farther away from the town (it now flows 1 km/¾ mile east of the town walls). The customs dues were finally abolished in 1796, during the French occupation.

The road enters Zons from the west. Nothing remains of the old town gate at this point, the Feldtor, but the imposing medieval walls and moat are well preserved. To the right is the South Tower (Südturm), which was converted into a windmill in the

Tour of the town

15th c. From here Schloss-strasse continues towards the Rhine. To the north (left) is the neo-Gothic church, built in 1875 on the site of an earlier 14th c. church. Beyond this, to the right, stands the Juddeturm or Jews' Tower (14th c., with a Baroque dome), at the corner of the outer ward of the castle, which served also to defend the castle against the town.

At the point where Schloss-strasse meets Rheingasse and the old riverside walls lay the old market place, with the town hall (not preserved) on the north side. To the right, in the old 17th c. manorhouse within the outer ward, is the District Museum (Kreismuseum), with an interesting collection of material on the history of the town (open Tuesday to Friday 2–6 p.m., Saturday and Sunday 10 a.m.–12.30 p.m. and 2–5 p.m.). To the south was the castle, of which there survive the double south gate leading into the outer ward, the gate-tower at the entrance to the castle itself and the tower at the south-east corner of the town walls.

Rheingasse is a picturesque and attractive little street with its old houses and the town walls looming over it. Just outside the walls, where the Rhine once flowed, cattle now graze. At the north end of Rheingasse is the square six-storied Rhine Tower or St Peter's Tower (Rheinturm, St-Peters-Turm), which once housed the customs post. On the inner side of the adjoining Rhine Gate (Rheintor) is a relief depicting Archbishop Friedrich von Saarwerden being granted the right to levy customs by St Peter, and below this is an inscription dated 1388 recording the construction of the gate. The tour ends with a walk along the town walls, passing a series of lookout posts and the Krötschenturm (completely preserved) at the north-west corner of the walls.

*Zoo, Aquarium and Insectarium   J/K10/11

Location
Riehler Strasse 178

U-Bahn
Zoo

Buses
134, 148

Trams
11, 15, 16

Cologne's large Zoo has over 6200 animals of some 665 species. Its Lemur House is unique, and it is famed for its collection of birds. In 1965 a jungle house for apes was opened. There are numerous open enclosures in which animals can live in conditions approximating to their natural habitat. A particular attraction is the Monkey Rock (Affenfelsen). There is also a Children's Zoo, in which children can stroke and feed the animals (but only with food from the slot machines provided). Facing the main entrance to the Zoo is the new building housing the Aquarium and Insectarium, with large numbers of insects, reptiles and fishes.

Opening times: summer daily 9 a.m.–6 p.m., winter daily 9 a.m.–5 p.m.; Aquarium daily 9.30 a.m.–6 p.m.

Practical Information

It is not always possible to give addresses and/or telephone numbers for all places listed in the Practical Information Section of these guides. This information is readily obtainable from hotel reception desks or from the local tourist office.

Airlines (local offices)

Air France
Richartz-Strasse 10, tel. 23 55 22
Airport, tel. 02203/40 21 60

Alitalia
Neumarkt 36, tel. 21 92 43
Airport, tel. 02203/40 25 28

British Airways
Marzellenstrasse 1, tel. 13 50 81
Airport, tel. 02203/40 22 29

Lufthansa
Bechergasse 16–32, tel. 82 68
Airport, tel. 02203/40 24 04

El Al
Wallrafplatz 9, tel. 21 09 51
Airport, tel. 02203/40 23 92

Japan Airlines
Burgmauer 16, tel. 23 44 58

KLM
Kaiser-Wilhelm-Ring 24, tel. 12 01 04
Airport, tel. 02203/40 22 60

Olympic Airways
Minoritenstrasse 7, tel. 23 61 38

Sabena
Burgmauer 10, tel. 21 90 21
Airport, tel. 02203/40 22 27

Swissair
Am Hof 16, tel. 2 02 51
Airport, tel. 02203/40 22 05

Airport

Cologne–Bonn Airport lies some 15 km/9 miles south-east of Cologne in the Wahner Heide.

Tel. 02203/40 22 22   Information

Bus 170 runs between the airport main building and the bus   Airport bus
terminal at the Central Station. The bus also stops at Köln-

115

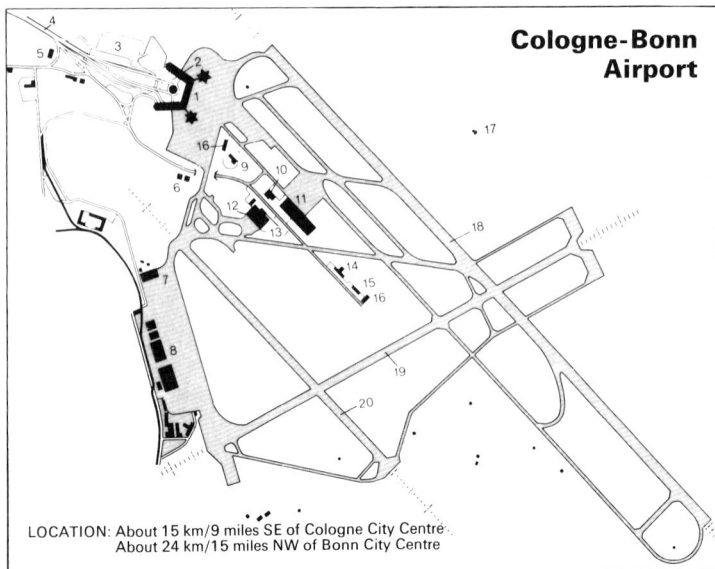

Cologne-Bonn Airport

LOCATION: About 15 km/9 miles SE of Cologne City Centre.
About 24 km/15 miles NW of Bonn City Centre

1 Passenger Terminal	7 General Aviation	13 Airport Administration Building
2 Central car park	8 Military sector of airport (old "Flower	14 Flight Security Building Control Tower
3 "North" car park	Airport" area)	15 Fire Brigade
4 Motorway to Cologne (Aachen, the Ruhr and	9 Fuel tanker compound	16 Equipment Hangar
Frankfurt-am-Main)	10 Lufthansa Service Company Building In-flight	17 Radar Tower
5 Airport hotel "Holiday Inn"	catering	18 Runway 14L/32R (3800 m/4157 yd)
6 Transformer compound; Emergency lighting	11 Air cargo	19 Runway 07/25 (2460 m/2691 yd)
compound	12 Aircraft hanger G1	20 Runway 14R/32L (1800 m/1969 yd)

Deutz Station on the right bank of the Rhine. The journey takes about 20 minutes. Buses run daily every 20 minutes from 6 a.m. to 10 p.m.
By using the autobahn the airport can be reached from Cologne in about 15 minutes.

"Airport Express"

There is a rail service, the "Airport Express", linking Düsseldorf Airport and Frankfurt Airport which calls at Köln-Deutz, Cologne Central Station and Bonn which is only for passengers with valid air tickets. It runs four times a day and is convenient for visitors to Cologne who arrive at Frankfurt Airport.

Money-changing

Deutsche Bank, Kreissparkasse (District Savings Bank)

Car rental

Autohansa, tel. 02203/40 21 42
Avis, tel. 02203/40 21 39
Europcar, tel. 02203/40 23 04
Hertz, tel. 02203/40 21 41
InterRent, tel. 02203/40 25 55
Sixt/Budget, tel. 02203/40 21 42
The car rental desks are situated near the central parking area (Zentralparkplatz)

Airport Hotel

Holiday Inn, Waldstrasse 255, tel. 02203/40 56 10. The hotel operates hotel courtesy transport.

Antiques

There are numerous antique shops in Cologne, many of them located in and around the city centre. Only a selection can be given here.

Abels (silver from 1600 to 1850), 5 Köln 41, Stadtwaldgürtel 32A

Antiquitäten – Asian Art, 5 Köln 1, Zeughausstrasse 10

Gil Antiquitäten (oak furniture and small objects), 5 Köln 30, Venloer Strasse 415

Hünerbein, Bernhard von (old musical instruments and graphic art), 5 Köln 1, Lintgasse 22

Interantik (period furniture of 17th, 18th and 19th c.), 5 Köln 1, Buttermarkt 22

Kunsthaus am Museum, Carola van Ham (art auctions, antiques, furniture, modern graphic art), 5 Köln 1, Drususgasse 1–5

Kunsthaus Brücke, M. Lambertz (furniture, silver, icons, pictures, Asiatica), 5 Köln 1, Quatermarkt 5

Kunsthaus Lempertz (renowned auctions; older, modern and East Asian art), 5 Köln 1, Neumarkt 3

Mondorf, A. (folk art), 5 Köln 1, Auf dem Rothenberg 9A–11

Sterzenbach, J. P. (furniture), 5 Köln 1, Lintgasse 5

Thiemann, M. (Art Nouveau, Art Deco), 5 Köln 1, Kettengasse 2

Art Galleries

Of Cologne's numerous galleries only a selection of the best known can be given here:

Gemälde-Galerie Abels (18th c. to Post-Impressionism), Stadtwaldgürtel 32A

Galerie Baukunst (works of Karl Hofer, 20th c. art) Theodor-Heuss-Ring 7

Galerie Boisserée am Wallraf-Richartz-Museum (old and modern graphic art, sculpture) Drususgasse 7–11

Galerie Dreiseitel (20th c. drawings, graphic art, etc.) Richmodstrasse 25

Kunsthandlung Goyert (old and contemporary graphic art, painting) Hahnenstrasse 18

117

Practical Information

Galerie Gmurzynska (avantgarde of the 1920s)
Obenmarspforten 21

Galerie Holtmann (international contemporary art)
Richartzstrasse 10

Kunsthandel Klefisch (non-European art, etc.)
Hardefustrasse 9

Naive-Kunst-Galerie Marianne Kühn (naive art)
Roteichenweg 5

Kunsthaus Lempertz (contemporary art)
Neumarkt 3

Kunsthaus am Museum Carola van Ham
Drususgasse 1/5

Galerie Orangerie – Reinz (contemporary art)
Helenenstrasse 2

Galerie Reckermann
Albertusstrasse 16

Galerie Ricke
Volksgartenstrasse 10

Galerie Ruchti (art of the present day)
Gertrudenstrasse 15

Galerie Runhof (naive art)
Filzengraben 19

Galerie Der Spiegel
Richartzstrasse 10

Galerie Stolz
Pferdmengesstrasse 30

Galerie Wentzel (art of the present day)
St-Apern-Strasse 26

Galerie Wilde (photographs)
Auf dem Berlich 6

Galerie Wintersberger+Kunst-Börse (contemporary art)
Kamekestrasse 21

Galerie Zwirner (art of the present day)
Albertusstrasse 18

The addresses of other galleries can be found in the "yellow
pages" telephone book under "Galereien"/"Kunstgalerien".

Banks

All the leading German banks have offices in Cologne.
Banking hours are Monday to Friday 8.30 a.m. to 1 p.m. and
2.30 to 4 p.m., Thursday until 5.30 p.m.

Camping and Caravanning

Campingplatz Berger, Uferstrasse 53A. In Köln-Rodenkirchen; open all year.

Campingplatz Waldbad, Peter-Baum-Weg. In Köln-Dünnwald; open all year.

Municipal Camp Site, Weidenweg 46. In Köln-Poll; open May 1 to October 10.

Youth Camping Site, Alfred-Schutte-Allee. In Köln-Poll; open July 1 to September 15.

As most sites become very crowded in the holiday season advance reservation is recommended, especially for visitors with caravans (trailers). The permission of the owner must first be obtained if you wish to camp on private land.

Details of all organised camp sites in the area can be obtained from the Tourist Information Bureau (tel. 33 45).

Information

See Information

Car rental

Avis, Clemensstrasse 29, tel. 23 43 33

AVS, Liebigstrasse 155, tel. 17 20 26–27

Hertz, Bismarckstrasse 19–21, tel. 51 50 84; at airport, tel. 02203/40 25 01

InterRent, Mindener Strasse 4, tel. 88 30 11; Luxemburger Strasse 181, tel. 44 10 47

The addresses of other firms can be found in the "yellow pages" telephone book under "Mietwagen".

Carnival

The Cologne Carnival (in German *Karneval*; in the local dialect *Fastelovend* or *Fastnacht*) Shrove Tuesday, the day before Ash Wednesday when the season of Lent begins, is for most of the people of the city a kind of "fifth season" of the year, a normal aspect of life. Visitors are likely to see the Carnival more as an explosive "happening". The origins of this event, during which the city is turned upside down, when the central area is closed to traffic and visitors may find themselves unwittingly involved in all kinds of unexpected situations, go back as far as the history of Cologne itself. The Carnival perpetuates the riotous Roman celebrations of the cult of Bacchus (the god of drunkenness and ecstasy) and the Saturnalia (Saturn being the god of farming and fertility); during these celebrations the normal order of things was suspended. The Carnival also

Carnival
(continued)

reflects old traditions of driving out the evil spirits of winter and celebrating the approach of spring. In those early days, however, the primary function of the Carnival was to act as a safety valve, for the release of popular energies in an explosion of high spirits.

The words *Fastnacht* and *Karneval* indicate the Christian interpretation given to the festival in the Middle Ages. During the carnival celebrations before the pre-Easter fast the people were able to have a last fling, so that during the forty days of Lent leading up to Easter they could behave in a decently restrained fashion. The word *Carnival* is derived from *Carne vale* ("meat, farewell"), the eating of meat being prohibited by the Church during the Lenten fast.

Not surprisingly the manifestations of high spirits during the Carnival were not always welcomed by the municipal authorities, and there are numerous examples down the centuries of edicts banning the wearing of masks and the rowdy activities of the participants.

The present organisation of the Carnival, with its processions and its "sittings" dates only from the 19th century, though it is based on earlier traditions. Thus during the Middle Ages members of guilds, family groups or the inhabitants of particular streets would form "bands" and, wearing masks, would parade through the streets to the accompaniment of music. The first "Rosen Montag" (*Rose Monday*) street procession, on the Monday before Ash Wednesday, was held in 1823. This has nothing to do with roses, *Rosen* being a corruption of *Rasen*, meaning "raving" or "mad". In the same year there first appeared the "Dreigestirn" (literally, "triple star") – the "big three" who hold sway in Cologne in carnival time. They are the "Prince", who featured in the 1823 procession as "Hero Carnival"; the "Maiden", who is played by a man and personifies, as "she" has since medieval times, the City of Cologne, the Roman *Colonia*; and the "Peasant", who represents the sturdy and sometimes rather vulgar ordinary citizen, but who is very conscious of his central role in the history of the city. He is depicted, for example, on the Eigelstein Gate (see A to Z, Romanesque Town Walls) holding the keys of the city which the citizens won from the archbishop in the Battle of Worringen in 1288.

The convivial drinking parties of earlier times and the "general assemblies" of the carnival organisers in the 19th century were the predecessors of the present-day "sittings" – events which include singing, dancing and comic speeches delivered from a wooden wash-tub! Another interesting event in this connection is the "Wolkenschieber" (*Lazybones*) Ballet, performed by the Cäcilia Wolkenburg Company (founded 1874), which perpetuates the tradition of the "divertissements" of the old Shrovetide dramatic performances. An important role in the carnival celebrations is played by the "Rote Funken" (*Red Sparks*, dating back to the city guard of 1660. They have appeared in the Rose Monday procession since its early days in the Romantic period, when its theme looked back to Cologne's great days as an Imperial Free City. The parody of the military is carried still further in the "Blaue Funken" (*Blue Sparks*), who wear the blue uniform of a Prussian regiment of dragoons. Another reminder of the city's history is provided by the "Reiiterkorps Jan von Werth" – *Jan von Werth's Cavalry Troop* (see A to Z, Rheinvorstadt, Jan von Werth Fountain). Another element of parody and inversion of the normal social order is

seen in the practice of throwing *Kamelle* (sweets) and
Strüüßcher (posies) from the carnival floats, aping as it does
the throwing of money and food to the populace by princes and
other high dignitaries in order to contribute to the carnival
mood.

Apart from the ''official'' Carnival, however, the traditional
Fastelovend (*Fast Evening*) is still celebrated in some of the
older parts of Cologne, with the same vigour and enthusiasm as
is shown in the organised Carnival events but with more
originality and imagination.

The Carnival begins on the Thursday before Ash Wednesday.
On this morning Cologne is taken over by the ''Jecken'' (*fools*
and the city's traffic is thrown into confusion. At 11 minutes
past 11 o'clock precisely the street carnival is officially opened
in the Old Market, and thereafter Cologne is ruled by women,
in a reversal of the normal social order, reminiscent of the
Roman Saturnalia. The women can flirt with any male and
generally play havoc with convention. Men wearing ties must
take care, for the women may try to cut them off!

At about 3 p.m. the carnival play ''Jan and Griet'' is performed
at the Severinstor (see A to Z, Roman City Walls).

Most offices and shops close in the afternoon, if they have not
already done so.

In the evening – and on the following evening – there are fancy-
dress balls and ''sittings'' (see above), held in various parts of
the city.

The Carnival calendar
Women's Carnival

About 11 a.m. the ''Red Sparks'' set up their encampment in the
Neumarkt. Processions are held in various parts of the city.

Carnival Saturday

About noon or at 1 p.m. processions, organised by schools and
by various quarters of the town start to parade through the city
centre which has now been closed to traffic. These processions, which began in 1933, hark back to the ''bands'' of earlier
days (see above).

Carnival Sunday

This is the climax of the Carnival. About midday the Rose
Monday Parade, with groups of dancers and musicians,
decorated floats, masked figures and the ''big three'' (Prince,
Maiden and Peasant), gets under way, the theme being set
each year by a particular slogan. Visitors are advised to
assemble as early as possible on the route of the procession,
since unofficial processions of ''Jecken'' often start out quite
early in the day as well. The Tourist Office can advise visitors of
the most convenient vantage points.

Rose Monday

About noon there are further unofficial processions in various
parts of the city.

Carnival Tuesday

''Am Aschermittwwoch, da ist alles vorbei'', in the words of the
song ''On Ash Wednesday it is all over''. In order to give
exhausted stomachs a rest and prepare their minds for Lent –
but also to keep the festivities going a little longer – friends meet
in the evening for a traditional fish meal.

Ash Wednesday

The opening of the Carnival ''session'' is actually celebrated in
Ostermann Platz by the Willi Ostermann Society on November
11 of the previous year (at 11 minutes past eleven o'clock on
the 11th day of the 11th month – eleven is a madman's lucky
number).

Other events

In the late afternoon of the same day the Senior Burgomaster officially opens the carnival season in the Town Hall.
In January the new "Prince" is proclaimed and between then and Carnival time a round of banquets, balls and not too serious processions heralds the approach of the Carnival proper for the citizens of Cologne.

Information

Information about the various parades and other events (including balls and "sittings" is given in the newspapers and in a brochure in several languages "Karnavel in Köln" (*Carnival in Cologne*) which is produced annually by the Tourist Office at the Cathedral.

Chemists (Pharmacies)

Night and emergency service

All chemists' shops display a notice giving the address and telephone number of chemists in the district who are open outside normal hours. Information about such chemists can also be obtained by dialling 11 50 (recorded announcement).

Cinemas (Movie Theaters)

To find what is on at Cologne's numerous cinemas, consult the newspapers or dial 1 15 11 (left bank of Rhine) or 1 15 14 (right bank).
Two specialised cinemas may interest some visitors:
Lupe 2, Neue Filmkunst Walter Kirchner, Mauritiussteinweg 102 (varied programme of older films).
Cinemathek in Wallraf-Richartz-Museum, An der Rechtsschule (regularly varied programme of less well known or more "advanced" films; retrospective shows of particular directors, actors or subjects).

Cultural institutes

Amerika-Haus, Apostelnkloster 13–15
Belgisches Haus, Cäcilienstrasse 46
British Council, Hahnenstrasse 6
Deutsch-Finnische Gesellschaft, c/o Finnische Abteilung, Institut für Nordische Philologie, Albertus-Magnus-Platz
Institut Français, Sachsenring 77
Italienisches Kulturinstitut, Universitätsstrasse 98
Japanisches Kulturinstitut, Universitätsstrasse 98
Jugoslavisches Zentrum, Hohenzollernring 49

Currency

In Germany the unit of currency is the Deutsche Mark (DM), divided in 100 Pfennige. There are bank notes for 10, 20, 50, 100, 500 and 1000 DM and coins for 1, 2 and 5 DM and 1, 5, 10 and 50 Pf.

Exchange rates

These fluctuate. In May 1987 they were approximately as follows: £1 = DM 2.9 and $1 = DM 1.77.

All banks in Coogne exchange foreign bank notes and travellers' cheques and cash Eurocheques. There are exchange offices at the airport and at the main railway station which remain open later than the banks and are also open at weekends. It is possible to change money at hotels and some larger stores, but the rates obtained are less favourable.

Changing money

Major credit cards, American Express, Diners Club, Access, Visa, etc. are widely accepted in Germany.

Credit cards

Customs Regulations

Visitors from a country belonging to the European Community may import free of duty the following: 300 cigarettes or 150 cigarillos or 75 cigars or 400 gr tobacco;
4 litres wine and $1\frac{1}{2}$ litres spirits over 22° Gay-Lussac (38·8° proof) or 3 litres fortified or sparkling wine up to 22° proof;
75 gr perfume and 0·375 litre toilet water, together with other goods to the value of DM500.

For visitors from non-EEC the amounts are 200 cigarettes or 100 cigarillos or 50 cigars or 250 gr tobacco (double if traveller does not reside in Europe). 2 litres wine and 1 litre of spirits or 2 litres of sparkling wine; 50 gr perfume and 0·25 litre toilet water.

If any of the above have been bought in a duty free shop the permitted amounts are approximately one third less; other goods are limited to a value of DM115. These reduced concessions also apply to visitors from other countries including the United States and Canada.

Doctors

For medical aid in an emergency dial 72 07 72. (Ärztlicher Notdienst).

Emergency calls

Police: dial 1 10

Fire: dial 1 12

Events

See Carnival

End February to early March

Flea market in old town on third Saturday in month

March–October

Easter Festival, usually in Deutz on right bank of Rhine.

April

Flower market in Old Market; (until beginning of September) music, floor show and dancing at Dancing Fountain, in Rheinpark, Deutz (Fri., Sat. and Sun.)
Junk market in Neumarkt (third weekend, beginning Fri.)
Wine Week in Neumarkt (end May to beginning of June)

May

Practical Information

June	Corpus Christi (Thurs after Trinity Sunday: Corpus Christi procession, with boats on Rhine) Organ recitals in Cathedral (Tues. at 8 p.m. until beginning of September)
July	Marksmen's Festival, Deutz International Summer Academy of the Dance
August	International Athletics Festival in Müngersdorf Stadium
September	International Pantomime Festival Junk market in Neumarkt (third weekend)
October	Horse racing: Preis von Europa at Weidenpesch
November	Carnival season opens on the 11th
December	Christmas Market in Neumarkt and old town Flea market in old town (Sundays in Advent) Six Day Cycle Race in Sporthalle (end December to beginning of January) Christmas cribs (Nativity groups) in Cologne churches (from 24th)
Trade fairs	See entry

Excursions

A booklet, issued by the Tourist Office at the cathedral (Unter Fettenhennen 19, tel. 33 45) entitled "Kölner Bummel Tips" gives a complete list of excursions and how to get there (U-Bahn/subway, tram/streetcar, buses, etc.). Among the more popular places are the Cologne Zoo and the Botanical Gardens in the suburb of Riehl, the Rhine Park which can be reached from the Zoo by cable-car across the river, the Wildgehege (wild animal park) and boat trips on the Rhine (see Rhine cruises).

Food and drink

Strictly speaking, Cologne has no distinctive cuisine of its own. This is not because, as a local saying puts it, "anything that comes on to the table is eaten", but rather because Cologne has from time immemorial been accustomed to enjoy a wide variety of culinary offerings, thanks to its far-flung trading connections and the numerous travellers who came to the town. There are, however, a number of dishes which can be regarded as Cologne specialties:

Typical dishes

Rheinischer Sauerbraten (braised pickled beef):
Beef pickled in a vinegar marinade, simmered in the marinade and onions and served with a sauce made of stock, raisins and cranberries, and accompanied by potato dumplings. This dish is claimed to taste better in Cologne than anywhere else.

Himmel und Ääd ("heaven and earth"):
A puree of potatoes (from the earth) and apples (from heaven),
served with fried blood sausage.

Hämcher (knuckle of pork):
Knuckles of pork, pickled and cooked in a vegetable stock;
accompanied by sauerkraut and puree, and eaten with plenty of
mustard.

Rievkooche (potato fritters):
Mashed potatoes, mixed with a little flour, grated onion and salt
and then fried in hot oil until they are crisp; eaten with black
bread and apple puree. Another dish which is said to taste
better in Cologne than anywhere else.

Halven Hahn ("half a cockerel"):
This is a sandwich or rye bread and mature Dutch cheese,
spread with mustard, which goes well with beer.

Kölschen Kaviar met Musik ("Cologne caviare with music"):
Another misleading name. This is a piece of blood sausage with
a rye bread roll and onions. The onions are the "music"
(because of the effects they produce during the digestive
process).

Wine and other beverages are drunk in Cologne, of course, but the real Cologne drink is the local top-fermented beer ("Kölsch"). | Drinks

Cologne-brewed beer, known in the local dialect as Kölsch, has a thousand years of tradition behind it and a reputation extending far beyond the bounds of the city. This beer, which has a very pleasant taste, is top-fermented (i.e. the yeast rises to the top during fermentation). Kölsch must be drunk chilled. It is served in tall slender glasses holding a fifth of a litre (just over a third of an Imperial pint), more than a billion of which are consumed annually. The best place to get it is one of the old Cologne breweries (see Restaurants), where the blue-aproned waiter (in Cologne dialect Köbes="Jacob") will bring a glass of cool beer as soon as he sees a customer arriving. | "Kölsch"

In recent years the top-fermented "white" beer known as Weiss has come back into favour. This is a rather cloudy beer from which the yeast has not been filtered out. | "Wiess"

Getting to Cologne

Good services operated mainly by British Airways and Lufthansa link the major airports of the UK with Cologne, the flight from London Heathrow or Gatwick taking about 1 hr 15 mins.
Cologne has good connections with the United States and Canada either direct or via Frankfurt (see Airport – "Airport Express"). | By air

The two principal routes from London are via Ostend and via the Hook of Holland. From London to Cologne via Ostend takes about 9 hours using Jetfoil and 12 hours on a | By rail

	conventional ferry. The day and night services from London via the Hook of Holland take 14 to 15 hours.
By road	Distances by road to Cologne: from Hook of Holland 278 km (173 miles); road E36 from Ostend 344 km (214 miles); road E5 from Bonn 17 km (10½ miles); road A555 from Frankfurt 217 km (135 miles); road E5 from Hannover 304 km (189 miles); road E73
Information	Full details about travel to Germany can be obtained from German National Tourist Board Offices in London, New York, Los Angeles, Montreal and Toronto. For addresses see Information.

Hotels

In the Federal Republic of Germany there is no official system of hotel classification, and accordingly the selection of hotels in this list, and the order in which they are listed, is based on general criteria. Luxury hotels are marked with an * asterisk.
*Inter-Continental, Helenenstrasse 14, 560 beds
*Excelsior Hotel Ernst, Trankgasse 1–5, 230 beds
*Dom-Hotel, Domkloster 2A, 184 beds
Holiday Inn, Waldstrasse 255, Köln 90, 160 beds
Crest Hotel, Dürener Strasse 287, 201 beds
Appartel Ambassador, Allerheiligenstrasse 2, 56 beds
Mondial, Bechergasse 10, 350 beds
Eden Hotel, Am Hof 18, 60 beds
Am Augustinerplatz, Hohe Strasse 30, 105 beds
Rheingold, Engelbertstrasse 33–35, 130 beds
Consul, Belfortstrasse 9, 160 beds
Ambassador, Barbarossaplatz 4A, 110 beds
Senats-Hotel, Unter Goldschmied 9–17, 80 beds
Drei Kronen, Auf dem Brand 6, 48 beds
Kosmos-Hotel, Waldeckerstrasse 11–15, 200 beds
Baseler Hof, Breslauer Platz 2, 156 beds
Kommerzhotel, Breslauer Platz, 75 beds
Bremer, Dürener Strasse 225–227, 99 beds
Best Western Hotel Regent, Melatengürtel 15, 270 beds
Königshof, Richartzstrasse 14–16, 135 beds
Esplanade, Hohenstaufenring 56, 60 beds
Bristol, Kaiser-Wilhelm-Ring 48, 59 beds
Imperial, Barthelstrasse 93, 65 beds
Haus Lyskirchen, Filzengraben 26–32, 83 beds
Windsor, von-Werth-Strasse 36–38, 56 beds
Coeliner Hof, Hansaring 98A–100, 87 beds
Merian-Hotel, Allerheiligenstrasse 1, 48 beds
Leonet, Rubensstrasse 33, 140 beds
Ludwig, Brandenburgerstrasse 22–24, 100 beds
Lenz, Ursulaplatz 9–11, 160 beds
Conti, Brüsseler Strasse 40–42, 86 beds
Buchholz, Kunibertgasse 5, 27 beds

Room booking service	The room booking service (Zimmernachweis) in the Tourist Office (tel. 2 22 33 45) is open on weekdays from 8 a.m. to 9 p.m., on Sundays and public holidays from 9.30 a.m. to 7 p.m. A fuller list of hotels, with tariffs, can be obtained there.

Information

Information of all kinds is provided by the Tourist Office at the
Cathedral (Unter Fettenhennen 19, tel. 33 45), which is open
Monday to Saturday from 8 a.m. to 9 p.m., on Sundays and
public holidays from 9.30 a.m. to 7 p.m.

For information by telephone dial the following numbers:

Cinema programmes, left bank of Rhine	1 15 11
right bank	1 15 14
Exhibitions, trade fairs, events in Cologne	1 15 16
News	1 16 5
Theatres and concerts	1 15 17
Weather for travellers	1 16 00

German National Tourist Board Overseas Offices:
61 Conduit Street, London W1R 0EN; tel. (01) 734 2600.   United Kingdom

747 Third Avenue,   United States
New York, NY 10017; tel. (212) 308 3300.
Broadway Plaza,
Suite 2230, 444 South Flower Street,
Los Angeles, CA 90017; tel. (213) 688 7332.

P.O. Box 417, 2 Fundy, Place Bonaventure,   Canada
Montreal, QUE. H5A 1B8;
tel. (514) 878 9885.
1290 Bay Street, Toronto, Ont. M5R 2C3;
tel. (416) 968 1570.

Libraries and archives

Central Library (Zentralbibliothek), Josef-Haubrich-Hof 1   Libraries

Central Medical Library (Zentralbibliothek der Medizin),
Josef-Stelzmann-Strasse 9

Chamber of Industry and Commerce Library (Bibliothek der
Industrie -und Handelskammer zu Köln), Unter Sachsenhausen 29–31

Diocesan Library (Diözesanbibliothek), Gereonstrasse 2–4:
church history of the Rhineland, theology, Dante collection

Evangelical library (Evangelische Bibliothek), Kartäusergasse 9

German Insurance Federation Library (Bibliothek des Ge-
samtverbandes der Deutschen Versicherungswirtschaft),
Ebertplatz 1

Institute of the German Economy Library (Bibliothek des
Instituts der Deutschen Wirtschaft), Gustav-Heinemann-Ufer
84–88: economic and social policy and history

Jewish Library (Germania Judaica), Josef-Haubrich-Hof 1: Jewish history and Jewish cultural history, the Third Reich

Municipal Museum Library (Bibliothek des Kölnischen Stadt-museums), Zeughausstrasse 1–3: history of the Rhineland, art and cultural history of Cologne

Theatre Museum Library (Theatermuseum des Instituts für Theater-Film- und Fernsehwissenschaften der Universität Köln, Bibliothek), 5 Köln 90 (Porz)

University and City Library (Universitäts- und Stadtbiblio-thek), Universitätsstrasse 33

Wallraf-Richartz Museum Library (Kunst- und Museums-bibliothek im Wallraf-Richartz-Museum), An der Rechts-schule: art history

Archives   Of the city's many archives only a selection can be listed here:

Economic Archives of Rhineland-Westphalia (Rheinisch-Westfälisches Wirtschaftsarchiv), Unter Sachsenhausen 29–31

Historical Archives of the Archbishopric of Cologne (His-torisches Archiv des Erzbistums Köln), Gereonstrasse 2–4

Historical Archives of the City of Cologne (Historisches Archiv der Stadt Köln), Severinstrasse 222–228: documents on the history of Cologne and official files

Joseph Haydn Institute, Blumenthalstrasse 23

Photo Archives of the Rhineland (Rheinisches Bildarchiv),

Unter Sachsenhausen 37: art and architectural history, particularly of the Rhineland

Lost property offices

General   Herkulesstrasse 42; tel. 1 77 11

Municipal transport   Property lost on U-bahn (subway), trams (streetcars) and buses: Scheidtweilerstrasse 38; tel. 54 71

Railway   Property lost on the railway:
Central Station, tel. 1 41 51 77
Deutz Station, tel. 1 41 55 65

Markets

Weekly markets   Altstadt-Mitte (Old Town, Centre), Alter Markt
Fri. 8 a.m.–6.30 p.m.

Altstadt-West (Old Town, West), Apostelnkloster
Tues. and Fri. 7 a.m.–1 p.m.

Junk market

Altstadt-Nord (Old Town, North), Sudermannplatz
Tues. and Fri. 7 a.m.–1 p.m.

Bickendorf, at swimming pool
Wed. and Sat. 7 a.m.–1 p.m.

Bocklemünd-Mengenich, Börnestrasse
Thurs. 7 a.m.–12.30 p.m.

Braunsfeld, Aachener Strasse/goods station
Tues., Thurs. and Sat. 7 a.m.–12.30 p.m.

Brück, Olpener Strasse/Am Gräfenhof
Tues. and Fri. 7 a.m.–12.30 p.m.

Brück, An St Adelheid
Thurs. 7 a.m.–12.30 p.m.

Buchforst, Waldecker Strasse
Wed. and Sat. 7 a.m.–1 p.m.

Buchheim, Elisabeth-Schäfer-Weg/Arnsberger Strasse
Fri. 7 a.m.–1 p.m.

Chorweiler, Pariser Platz
Thurs. 7 a.m.–12.30 p.m.

Dellbrück, Kemperbachstrasse
Thurs. 7 a.m.–12.30 p.m.

Practical Information

Weekly markets
(continued)

Deutz, under Severinsbrücke
Tues. and Fri. 7 a.m.–12.30 p.m.

Ehrenfeld, Neptunplatz
Tues. and Fri. 7 a.m.–1 p.m.

Ensen/Westhoven, Gilgaustrasse
Sat. 7 a.m.–1 p.m.

Flittard, Einsteinstrasse/Eduard-Heis-Strasse
Thurs. 7 a.m.–12.30 p.m.

Heimersdorf, Haselnusshof
Wed. and Sat. 7 a.m.–12.30 p.m.

Höhenhaus, Wupperplatz
Wed. and Sat. 7 a.m.–12.30 p.m.

Humboldt/Gremberg, Gremberger Strasse/Taunusstrasse
Thurs. 7 a.m.–1 p.m.

Klettenberg, Siebengebirgsallee/Gürtel
Wed. and Sat. 7 a.m.–1 p.m.

Lindenthal, Gleueler Strasse/Gürtel
Tues. and Fri. 7 a.m.–1 p.m.

Longerich, Schlackstrasse/Johannes-Rings-Strasse
Wed. and Sat. 7 a.m.–12.30 p.m.

Mülheim, Schützenplatz/Beliner Strasse
Tues. and Fri. 7 a.m.–1 p.m.

Mülheim, Stegerwaldsiedlung/An St Urban
Wed. and Sat. 7 a.m.–12.30 p.m.

Niehl, Waldfriedhofstrasse
Thurs. 7 a.m.–1 p.m.

Nippes, Wilhelmplatz
Mon., Tues., Wed., Thurs., Fri. and Sat. 7 a.m.–1 p.m.

Poll, Siegburger Strasse/Rolshover Strasse
Fri. 7 a.m.–1 p.m.

Porz, Friedrich-Ebert-Platz
Tues. and Sat. 7 a.m.–1 p.m.

Porz-Urbach, Am Schwanenbitzer Hof
Thurs. 7 a.m.–1 p.m.

Riehl, Garthestrasse/Gürtel
Wed. and Sat. 7 a.m.–1 p.m.

Rodenkirchen, Maternusplatz
Sat. 7 a.m.–1 p.m.

Stammheim, Moses-Hess-Strasse
Thurs. 7 a.m.–12.30 p.m.

Sülz, Auerbachplatz
Tues. and Fri. 7 a.m.–1 p.m.

Sülz, Hermeskeiler Platz
Tues. and Fri. 7 a.m.–12.30 p.m.

Vingst, Ostheimer Strasse/Siegrid-Undset-Strasse
Tues. and Fri. 7 a.m.–1 p.m.

Weiden, Emil-Schreiterer-Platz
Wed. and Sat. 7 a.m.–1 p.m.

Zollstock, Höninger Weg/Herthastrasse
Thurs. 7 a.m.–1 p.m.

Flea markets are held from May to October in the Old Market (Alter Markt), the Southern Sports Complex (Sportanlage Süd), the Nippes quarter and the Ladenstadt shopping centre near the Opera (see Events).
Junk markets, flower markets and Christmas markets: see Events.

Flea markets

Money-changing

See Currency

Museums

Applied Art, Museum of
See A to Z, Overstolz House

Museums described in the A to Z section

Diocesan Museum
See A to Z, Diocesan Museum

El-De-Haus,
See A to Z, El-De-Haus

Ethnology, Museum of
See A to Z, Rautenstrauch-Joest Museum

Ludwig Museum
See A to Z, Wallraf-Richartz-Museum and Ludwig Museum

Municipal Museum
See A to Z, Arsenal

Rautenstrauch-Joest Museum
See A to Z, Rautenstrauch-Joest Museum

Roman-Germanic Museum
See A to Z, Roman-Germanic Museum

Schnütgen Museum
See A to Z, Schnütgen Museum

Wallraf-Richartz-Museum
See A to Z, Wallraf-Richartz and Ludwig Museum

Practical Information

Zons District Museum
See A to Z, Zons.

Other museums

Brewing Museum,
Küppers-Kölsch-Brauerei,
Alteburger Strasse, Köln-Bayenthal, tel. 3 77 91
Open Sat. 11 a.m.–4 p.m.

Cutlery Museum (Besteck-Museum Bodo Glaub),
Burgmauer 68, tel. 13 41 36
Open Tues.–Fri. 3–6 p.m., Sat. 11 a.m.–2 p.m.

Forest Museum (Waldmuseum),
Gut Leidenhausen, Köln-Porz, tel. 2 21 30 43
Open Sun. 10 a.m.–5 p.m.

German Sports Museum
(under construction)

Herbig-Haarhaus Lacquer Museum (Lackmuseum),
Vitalisstrasse 198–226, tel. 5 88 11
East Asian and European lacquerware
Seen by appointment Mon.–Thurs. 9 a.m.–4 p.m. and Fri.
9 a.m.–noon

Motor Museum (Motorenmuseum) of the Klöckner-
Humboldt-Deutz Co.,
Deutz, Mülheimer Strasse 107, tel. 8 22 29 18
Examples of engines, including the world's first four-stroke
engine, produced by N. Otto in Cologne in 1876
Open Mon.–Fri. 9 a.m.–4 p.m.
Conducted tours by arrangement

Museum of the Geological Institute of Cologne University,
Zülpicher Strasse 49, tel. 4 70 22 62
Open October to mid July, Wed. 10 a.m.–6 p.m. and by
arrangement

Museum of Holography (Holographiemuseum),
Pletschmühlenweg 7, Pulheim bei Köln, tel. 02238/5 10 54
Three-dimensional images produced by laser beams
Open Fri. 2–8 p.m., Sat. and Sun. 11 a.m.–6 p.m.

Theatre Museum,
Theaterwissenschaftliches Institut der Universität Köln,
Burg Wahn, Köln-Porz, tel. 02203/6 41 85
Seen by appointment only

Music

Major concerts take place in the new Philharmonic Hall,
including performances by the two principal orchestras of
Cologne, the Gürzenich and the West German Radio Symphony Orchestra.

Gürzenich Municipal Orchestra
Box office (day): Offenbachplatz 1
Box office (evening): Gürzenich, Martinstrasse 29–31

Rhineland College of Music (Rheinische Musikschule)
Vogelsanger Strasse 28

Rhineland Chamber Orchestra (Rheinisches Kammer-orchester)
Steinfeldergasse 11

Sartory Halls (Sartory-Säle: various events)
Friesenstrasse 44

State College of Music (Staatliche Hochschule für Musik)
Dagobertstrasse 38

West German Radio (Westdeutscher Rundfunk: symphony orchestra, etc.)
Wallrafplatz 5, tel. 2 20 21 44; Funkhaus (Radio House), Appellhofplatz 1

Programmes (and the addresses of other concert halls) are given in the newspapers and in a brochure ("Monats-vorschau", "The Month Ahead") issued by the Tourist Office (which also lists recitals in Cologne churches).

Programmes

Opera House, Offenbachplatz 1
Programme: in newspapers and monthly magazines, on many advertising columns, by telephone (dial 1 15 17 for recorded announcements) and in the Tourist Office's "Monats-vorschau".

Opera

Newspapers

The first forerunners of our modern newspapers – broadsheets giving the news of the day – appeared in Cologne in 1572. 1588 saw the first appearance of the "Messrelationen", published twice yearly with information about trade fairs. In 1734 Johann Ignaz Roderique, publisher of the "Gazette de Cologne", attacked Frederick the Great of Prussia in his paper, so incensing the king that he paid a hit man 100 guilders to beat him up. The "Kölnische Zeitung", founded in 1798, was acquired in 1802 by the printing house of G. A. Schauberg, which in 1805 passed by marriage to Markus DuMont; and the firm of DuMont-Schauberg have been the publishers since 1876 of the "Stadtanzeiger".
The "Rheinische Zeitung" which appeared in 1843 was edited by Karl Marx until its banning by the Prussian censor. In 1894 it reappeared as an organ of the Social Democratic Party; after being banned by the Nazis in 1933 it was allowed by the Allied authorities to reappear in 1946, but finally ceased publication in 1974.
The conservative and Catholic "Kölnische Zeitung" was founded by the publishing house of Bachem in 1860.
The paper with the largest circulation is now the popular tabloid "Express" (DuMont-Schauberg), 380,000 copies), followed by the "Stadtanzeiger" (also DuMont, 270,000 copies) and the "Kölnische Rundschau" (180,000 copies).
For information about events and entertaiments and local news the following monthly publications will be found useful: "Köln im . . . Das Kölner Monatsjournal", published by the Alfred-

Practical Information

Beck-Verlag, with forthcoming events, discussions of restaurants and books, etc.;

"Stadtrevue" (left-wing), with forthcoming events, advertisements, current topics, discussions of restaurants, etc.;

"Schauplatz" (also left-wing), a competitor to the "Stadtrevue", on similar lines.

Night life

Three areas of Cologne in particular have a concentration of bars, restaurants, night spots, etc., catering for pretty well every taste:

Old town (Altstadt: the Martinsviertel, between the Alter Markt and Neumarkt and the Rhine): plenty of variety, romantic atmosphere, but overcrowded.

Around the Hohenzollernring and farther in: mainly night spots and discotheques.

On both sides of Zülpicher Strasse between the Ring and the railway bridge: the students' quarter, with discotheques, etc.

Information

Fuller information, with recommendations, is given in a booklet issued by the Tourist Office at the Cathedral, "Bummeltips zwischen Rhein und Ring".

Opening times

Shops

Most shops open in the morning between 8 and 9.30 a.m. and close between 6 and 6.30 p.m. Some shops, particularly in the outer districts, close for lunch between 1 and 3 p.m. On Saturday most shops shut at 2 p.m., but on the first Saturday in the month ("Long Saturday") and on the four weekends before Christmas stay open until 6 p.m. (though shops in the outer districts may close earlier).

Museums

The opening times of museums and other places of interest are given in the individual A to Z entries.

Churches

Most churches are open throughout the day (usually closing at dusk), but some close at lunchtime.

Postal services

Head Post Office

Hauptpostamt, An den Dominikanern 4: open Mon.–Fri. 8 a.m.–6p.m., Sat. 8 a.m.–1 p.m.

Night services

In Head Post Office: Mon.–Fri. 6 p.m. to 8 a.m., Sat. 10 p.m. to 8 a.m., Sun. 10 p.m. to 7 a.m.

In Central Station

Post office open daily 7 a.m. to 10 p.m.

Other post offices

Same opening times as the Head Post Office, but no night services. Some close at lunchtime from noon to 3 p.m.

Public holidays

The following public holidays are observed in Cologne: New
Year's Day, Good Friday, Easter Monday, 1 May, Ascension,
Whit Monday, Corpus Christi, German Unity Day (17 June),
Day of Prayer and Repentance, All Saints (1 November),
24 and 25 November.
In addition there are the Carnival holidays in February/March
(see Carnival). On the Thursday before Carnival many shops
and all offices close, at least in the afternoon, and on Rose
Monday many shops are open only for a few hours in the
morning. Museums are closed over the Carnival period.

Public transport

The Cologne area is divided into a number of concentric zones,
and the fare depends on the number of zones traversed in the
course of a journey. As a general rule visitors will be concerned
only with the central zone, which coincides broadly with the
city limits and is the equivalent of two normal zones. Such
places as Bergisch-Gladbach, Hürth/Brühl and Leverkusen lie
outside the central zone, and each of them involves travelling
through three zones. There is a direct line to Bonn (No. 16:
6 zones).

Tariff zones

At U-Bahn (Underground) stations and other stations and
stopping places marked with a V (i.e. broadly those in the
central area) tickets are obtained from ticket machines, **not** on
the train, bus or tram. Elsewhere tickets (single journey tickets
only) are bought from the driver. There are also ticket offices at
the Dom/Hauptbahnhof, Neumarkt and Ebertplatz U-Bahn
stations and at Scheidtweilerstrasse 38, Braunsfeld.

Sale of tickets

Visitors will find it well worth while to invest in a 24-hour ticket,
valid on all services within the particular zone from midnight to
midnight. Tickets can be bought at the usual ticket offices.

24-hour tickets

A two-city ticket, valid for 24 hours, allows the holder to use
tram, bus and rail services in any two of the following transport
areas: Berlin, Bonn, Bremen, Cologne, Frankfurt, Hamburg,
Hannover, Mannheim/Ludwigshafen, Munich, Nürnberg/
Fürth, Rhine/Ruhr, Stuttgart.
These tickets can be bought at the larger railway stations and
official travel agencies.

Two-city tickets

Tickets must be validated by cancellation in a cancelling
machine on the bus or tram (on the U-Bahn at the barrier before
getting into the train).

Validation of tickets

The Köln–Bonner Eisenbahn (KBE) runs between Cologne and
Bonn, calling at Brühl and other intermediate stations. The
station in Cologne is in Barbarossaplatz.

Köln–Bonner Eisenbahn
(Cologne–Bonn Railway)

The shortage of parking space in the city centre makes it
advisable for visitors coming in from outside the city to use the

"Park and ride"

135

Plan of the Cologne Public Transport Undertaking and the Cologne-Bonn Railways

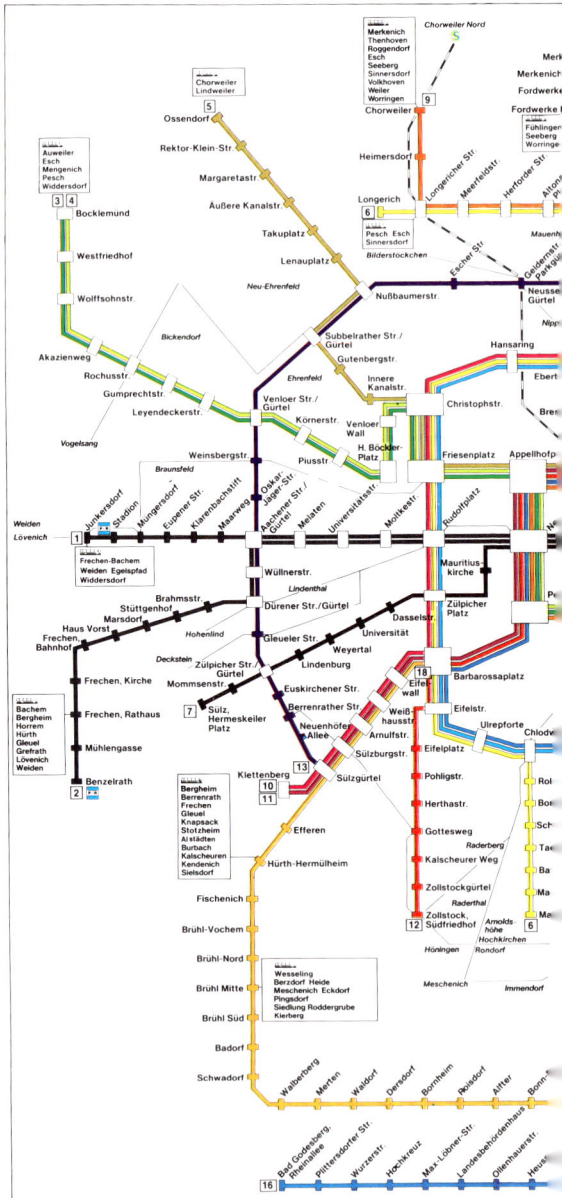

Schlebusch **4**
Odenthaler Str.
Stammheim
Bruder-Klaus-Siedlung Dünnwald Leuchtstr.
Stammheim Flittard
Bayerwerk Leverkusen Am Emberg
Kuppersteg Opladen
10 Fixheider Weg
Fordwerke
Ölhafen
Neurather Ring **11** Höhenhaus
Fordwerke Süd
Rixdorfer Str.
Geestemünder Str. Höhenhaus, Birkenweg
Dünnwald Am Donewald
Niehl Von-Sparr-Str.

Wilhelm-Sollmann-Str. Keupstr.
Weidenpesch
Scheibenstr. Holweide
Moll- **13** Mülheim Mülheimer Ring Herler Ring Maria-Himmelfahrt-Str. Neufelder Str. Dellbrück Mauspfad Bergisch Gladbach
witzstr. Wiener Platz
Florastr. **16** Brücke Buchheim Dellbrück, Hauptstr. **15**
Boltensternstr. Wichheimer Str. Thielenbruch **3**
Lohsestr. **5** Zoo Grünstr. Herler Str.
Buchforst Frankfurter Str.
Reichenspergerplatz Waldecker Str. Bensberg **1**
Riehl Niehl Stegerwaldsiedlung Kölner Str.
Neuenweg
Dom/Hbf. Hohenzollern Messe/ Höhenberg Frankenforst
brücke Sporthalle Kippekausen
Deutzer Freiheit Bf Deutz/ Kalk Post Kalk Kapelle Fuldaer Str. Frankfurter Str. Kalker Friedhof Merheim Fliehbachstr. Refrath
Heumarkt Deutzer Str. Messe Deutz-Kalker Bad Lustheide
Waidmarkt Brücke Brück, Mauspfad
Severinstr. Severins- Deutz-Kalker Str. Neu-Brück
brücke Suevenstr. Humboldt
Severinsbrücke Gremberg Vingst
Drehbrücke Ostheim **2**
Eiche/Rosenstr. Poller Kirchweg Autobahn
Südbrücke Steinweg
Ubierring Krückelstr. Porzer Str.
Schönhauser Str. Poll Poll, Salmstr. Rath-Heumar
Bayenthalgürtel Poll, Autobahn Röttgensweg
Marienburg Gremberghoven Königsforst
Rodenkirchen Westhoven, Kölner Str. **9**
Siegstr. Weiß Westhoven, Berliner Str.
Michaelshoven Ensen, Gilgaustr. Eil
Sürth Ensen, Kloster
Godorf Elsdorf Porz, Steinstr.
Wesseling Nord Flughafen Urbach
Wesseling Köln/Bonn Porz, Markt
Wesseling Süd Grengel Porz, Glaswerke
Urfeld Libur Lind Wahn Wahnheide
Widdig Zündorf **7**
Uedorf Langel Lind Lülsdorf Ranzel Niederkassel Rheidt Mondorf Sieglar Wahnheide Wahn
Hersel
Buschdorf
Tannenbusch Mitte **KVB**
Tannenbusch Süd **KBE**
18 Bonn Rheinuferbahnhof
Hauptbahnhof (ZOB) Rail & Tram Important Bus connections
Universität/Markt Riehl - municipal S S-Bahn - Railways
Juridicum participation
Bus service Park & Ride
City Centre - Airport

Kölner Verkehrs-Betriebe
Köln-Bonner Eisenbahnene
Scheidtweilerstr. 38
5000 Köln 41 (Braunsfeld)
Tel. (0221) 5471

Passenger Information:
Tel. (0221) 547 3333

Cologne-Bonn Airport

137

"park and ride" system, leaving their car on the outskirts of the city and continuing by tram. The following tram stops have park and ride facilities, with signs indicating this:
From the north: Neusser Strasse/Gürtel: routes 6, 9, 10, 12 and 13.
From the north and, using the urban motorway, from the east and south: Zoo: routes 4, 11 and 15.
From the east and south: Severinsbrücke: route 7.
From the west: Stadion: route 1.
From the south: Sürth or Rodenkirchen: routes 15 and 16.

Rhine cableway
(Rheinseilbahn)

This 920 m/1000 yd long cableway carries passengers from the Trade Fair Grounds over the Rheinpark and the Rhine to the Zoo. It operates from Easter to the end of October, Saturday to Thursday, continuously from 10 a.m. to 7 p.m.

Puppet Theatre (Puppenspiele)

Cologne's Puppet Theatre, or "Hännesje-Theater", was founded in 1802 by a tailor named Christoph Winters. The main characters in the plays performed here are Hännesje (a diminutive of Johannes or John), a wily and disrespectful but basically goodhearted rogue; Bärbelchen (Diminutive of Barbara), his quick-witted girl friend; Besteva (Grandpa) and his wife Maritzebill (Maria Sibylla); their neighbour Tünnes (Anton), also known as "de Nas" (the Nose) because of his large red nose; and Speimanes, the "Spitter", who stutters and splutters as he speaks. The characters speak in a modified version of the Cologne dialect ("Kölsch") – though even a modified version may not be easy for foreigners to understand. Address of the Puppet Theatre: Eisenmarkt (tel. 21 20 95).

Radio and television

West German Radio
(Westdeutscher Rundfunk,
WDR)

The West German Radio Company began transmitting its programmes from Cologne in 1926, after the Allied occupation authorities had lifted the ban on radio transmissions in the Rhineland. From 1945 to 1955 it was permitted to operate only as part of North-West German Radio and subject to regulations laid down by the occupying powers. It again became independent in 1955.

Radio programmes

West German Radio in Cologne now transmits four programmes:
1st programme (in common with North German Radio): news, music and entertainment.
2nd programme: information, traffic news, magazine programmes (e.g. the Morning and Lunchtime Magazines) and entertainment.
3rd programme: music and the spoken word (quality programmes).
4th programme: broadcasting of Parliamentary debates, educational programmes, foreign language transmissions.

Television

With some 1000 hours of television a year, West German Radio is the largest of the nine broadcasting organisations included in the Federal Republic's network and provides 25 per cent of the networked programmes. It also transmits a regional programme (with advertising), the Third Programme (WDR III), with 3000 hours on the air annually, and the West German school television service.

The Federal Republic's world service, the Deutsche Welle ("German Wave"), was originally established in 1929, and became an independent corporation in 1960. Its programmes are transmitted on short waves throughout the 24 hours and can be heard anywhere in the world in three transmissions every day. In 33 languages as well as German, they report on politics, economic affairs and culture in the Federal Republic.

World service

Deutschlandfunk (Radio Germany), established in 1960, transmits programmes in German and 11 other languages on long and medium waves for the information of European listeners.
The Deutsche Welle and Deutschlandfunk have had their headquarters since 1979 in a new building on Raderberggürtel, on the south side of the city.

European service

Rail travel

In Central Station, tel. 27 61

General information

To Hamburg and North Germany: tel. 1 15 33
To Hannover and Central Germany: tel. 1 15 34
To Frankfurt and Nürnberg: tel. 1 15 35
To Munich and Austria: tel. 1 15 36
To Basle and Saarbrücken: tel. 1 15 37

Timetable information

Central Station, tel. 13 41 15, 13 49 83

Express freight

Deutz Station, tel. 1 41 56 66

Motorail

Tel. 1 41 55 29

Seat reservations

Tel. 1 41 51 60

Special trains, group travel

Tel. 1 41 51 77

Lost property

Railway stations

Cologne's Central Station (Hauptbahnhof) is just beside the Cathedral in the centre of the city. It can be reached by the following public transport services:
Trams: 5, 9, 11, 12, 16
Buses: 132, 133, 170 (Airport)
When required there are special services to and from the Trade Fair Grounds (No. 149).

Central Station

Left luggage office, luggage lockers, post office, bank, restaurants, Railway Mission, cinema, bookshop, German and international newspapers and periodicals, tobacconist, flower shop, souvenirs, lost property office, (carrying both cars and their passengers to distant holiday areas).

Services available in Central Station

The most important of Cologne's other stations is the one in Deutz, in Ottoplatz, just beside the Trade Fair Grounds. This is the arrival and departure point of the motorail service, (carrying both cars and their passengers to distant holiday areas).

Restaurants

German restaurants	Goldener Pflug, Olpener Strasse 421
	Franz Kellers Restaurant, Aachener Strasse 21
	St Georg, Blaubach 18
	Bastei, Konrad-Adenauer-Ufer 80
	Weinhaus Im Walfisch, Salzgasse 13
	Börsenrestaurant, Unter Sachsenhausen 10–26
	Ratskeller, Rathausplatz 1
	Marienbild, Aachener Strasse 561
	Wolff, Komödienstrasse 50–52
French restaurants	Restaurant Bado La Poêle d'Or, Komödienstrasse 52
	Chez Alex, Mühlengasse 1
	Auberge de la Charrue d'Or, Habsburger Ring 18
	Chez Laurent, Eifelstrasse 33
	Sigi's Bistro, Kleiner Griechenmarkt 23–25
	La Baguette, Heinsbergstrasse 20
Italian restaurants	Bei Rino Fontana di Trevi, Ebertplatz 3–5
	Ristorante Grand'Italia, Hansaring 66
	Luciano, Marzellenstrasse 68
	Sansone, Händelstrasse 47
	Ristorante Alfredo, Tunisstrasse 3
Typical Cologne beer-houses	Altstadt-Päffgen, Heumarkt 62
	Brauereu Zur Malzmühle, Heumarkt 6
	Brauhaus Sion, Unter Taschenmacher 5–7
	Em Goldene Kappes, Neusser Strasse 295
	Haus Töller, Weyerstrasse 96
	Hofbräu Früh, Am Hof 12–14
	Päffgen, Friesenstrasse 64
	Schmitze Lang, Severinstrasse 62
Restaurants open all night	Drachenburg-Keller, Heumarkt 50
	Mager Klaus, Friesenstrasse 58
	Wicküler im Römer, Kleine Budengasse 1–3
Hotel restaurants	See Hotels

Rhine cruises

Cruises on the Rhine are operated by the following companies; they can be booked through the Tourist Office at the Cathedral:
Köln-Düsseldorfer Deutsche Rheinschiffahrt (AG), Frankenwerft 15, tel. 2 08 80.
Rhein-Mosel Personenschiffahrt, Konrad-Adenauer-Ufer, tel. 12 16 00.
Dampfschiffahrt Colonia, Buttermarkt 33, tel. 21 13 25.

Shopping

Cologne's principal shopping area is in the city centre, in the Hohe Strasse/Schildergasse pedestrian precinct and around Breite Strasse/Ehrenstrasse and Mittelstrasse.

Sightseeing tours

City tours, conducted tours for parties and excursions in the surrounding area can be booked through the Tourist Office at the Cathedral (Unter Fettenhennen 19, tel. 2 21 33 45). There are very many possibilities – coach tours of Cologne, "an evening in Cologne", a guided tour on foot, etc.

Sports

In addition to the main stadium (with covered seating for 60,000) – a multi-purpose arena which is not only the headquarters of the Cologne football team but also accommodates such diverse events as athletic meetings, the Cathedral Jubilee in 1980 and a concert by the Rolling Stones in 1982 – the Müngersdorf complex also includes a riding school, a hockey field, tennis courts, a swimming pool and other sports facilities. The German Academy of Sport (Deutsche Sporthochschule) is also in this area.

Müngersdorf Stadium, Aachener Strasse

The facilities at Lentstrasse comprise an indoor ice rink (seating for 6000), an outdoor rink, a swimming pool, a sauna and a solarium. This is the headquarters of the Cologne ice hockey team.

Ice and Swimming Stadium (Eis- und Schwimmstadion), Lentstrasse

This artificial lake, created in an old lignite mine, offers a variety of recreational facilities for water sports, including a 2300 m/ 2500 yd course for canoe and rowing races.

Fühlinger See, Stallagsbergweg

This multi-purpose hall (seating for 7700), with a cycle-racing track, which is used not only for sporting events (e.g. six-day races) but for concerts and other non-sporting events.

Sporthalle, Deutz–Mülheimer Strasse

A multi-purpose stadium used for football (Fortuna Cologne), American football (Cologne Crocodiles), athletics and various indoor forms of sport.

South Stadium (Stadion Süd), Vorgebirgstrasse

The most important of the horse races held here are the Preis von Europa (Europe Prize), the Gerling Prize, the Union Race and the Winter Favourite Prize.

Weidenpesch Racecourse, Rennbahnstrasse/ Scheibenstrasse

There are facilities for tennis and squash at Brücker Sportpark, Oberberbruchweg 6, at City-sport, Rhöndorferstrasse 10 and at several other places. There are golf courses at Marienburg (9 holes) and at Refrath (18 holes). Information on all sporting matters can be obtained from the Sportamt der Stadt Köln, Aachenerstrasse, Stadion, D-5000 Köln 41, tel. 4 98 31.

Swimming pools

Open-air pools	Brück, Hovenstrasse Fühlinger See, Stallagsbergweg Müngersdorf Stadium, Aachener Strasse Vingst, Vingster Ring
Indoor pools (a selection)	Agrippabad, Kämmergasse 1 Deutz-Kalker Bad, Deutz-Kalker Strasse, tel. 54 22 19 13 12 Genovevabad, Bergisch-Gladbacher Strasse, tel. 67 61 32 91 Marsiliusbad, Nikolausstrasse 55 Neptunbad, Neptunplatz 1
Thermal baths	Kurbad Marienburg, Marienburger Strasse 70 Martinsbad, Lintgasse 10–14 Kurbad am Stadtwald, Hültzstrasse 21 Thermalbad im Rheinpark, Sachsenbergstrasse

Television

See Radio and television

Theatres

	Schauspielhaus (drama and comedy), Offenbachplatz Werkstattbühne Schlosserei (Theatre Workshop), Krebsgasse Kammerspiele, Ubierring 45 Theater am Dom, Ladenstadt (modern drama), Breite Strasse Theater "Der Keller" (experimental drama), Kleingedank-strasse 6 Theater Kefka (Pantomime), Aachener Strasse 24 "Die Machtwächter" (Cabaret), Gertrudenstrasse 24 Volkstheater Millowitsch, Aachener Strasse 5 Theater "Im Vringsveedel", Severinstrasse 81 Senftöpfchen, Pipinstrasse 2 Theater OFF-OFF, Industriestrasse 170 Studiobühne der Universität (University Studio Theatre), Universitätsstrasse 16 Atelier-Theater, Roonstrasse 78 Puppenspiele, see entry Puppet Theatre
Programmes	To see what's on, consult the newspapers or monthlies, or the brochure issued by the Tourist Office, "Monatsvorschau" ("The Month Ahead").
Ticket agencies	Theaterkasse am Neumarkt (in pedestrian underpass) tel. 21 43 32 Theaterkasse im Kaufhof (Hohe Strasse) tel. 21 66 92 Theaterkasse am Rudolfplatz, tel. 24 69 45 Theaterkasse am Ebertplatz (in Reisebüro Hartmann, corner of Neusser Strasse) tel. 73 70 00

Time

Germany is on Central European Time (Mitteleuropaische Zeit – MEZ), one hour ahead of Greenwich Mean Time and six hours ahead of Eastern Standard Time. Summer Time (Daylight Saving) is two hours ahead of Greenwich Mean Time and seven hours ahead of Eastern Standard Time.

Tipping

A service charge is usually included in hotel and restaurant bills; tipping is therefore at the discretion of the customer. It is usual to tip the usherette at a cinema or theatre, a lavatory attendant, taxi drivers and guides, plus porters, bellhops, and doormen.

Trade fairs

The following trade fairs (some of them open only to the trade) are held periodically in Cologne at the times given:

International Furniture Fair (annually)	January
International Confectionery Fair (annually)	January/February
Domotechnika (domestic electrical appliances and equipment, domestic technology: annually)	February
International Men's Fashion Week and International Jeans Fair (twice a year)	February/August
International Children and Young People (Kind und Jugend) Fair (twice a year)	March/September
West German Art Fair (antiques: in odd-numbered years) Ironware (annually)	March
International Needlework Fair (even-numbered years)	April/May
Optica (International Optical Fair: in even-numbered years) Interzum (furniture, interior decoration: in odd-numbered years)	May
Inatec (International Food Technology Congress and Fair: in odd-numbered years)	May/June
Ifcom/Telecom (Telecommunications Congress and Show: in odd-numbered years)	June
Spoga (sports equipment, camping gear, garden furniture: annually) Gardens Fair (annually) IFMA (International Cycle and Motorcycle Show: in even-numbered years) s + b (sport, bathing and recreational facilities: in odd-numbered years)	September
Photokina (photographic and film technology: in even-numbered years)	September/October

October	Anuga (World Food Fair: in odd-numbered years) Orgatechnik (office and business equipment: in even-numbered years)
October/November	Modelmaking Fair (even-numbered years) International Art Fair (odd-numbered years)
Information	Further information can be obtained from Kölnmesse Messe und Ausstellungs-GmbH, Postfach 21 07 60, 5 Köln 21, tel. 82 11 and from Tourist Agencies.

Travel Documents

Passports	British subjects require either a full passport or a visitor's passport to enter West Germany. No visa is required. US and Canadian Citizens require a full passport but no visa.
Motoring Documents	A national or international driving licence and car registration papers are required for British visitors. Citizens of the US and Canada must have a national or international driving permit and an international certificate for motor vehicles. Every foreign car must display the appropriate international distinguishing sign.
Insurance	Third party insurance is compulsory. Foreign visitors, other than nationals of EEC countries, must have either a green card or take out third party insurance at the frontier. It is advisable to take out adequate medical and general travel insurance before leaving home.

Youth hostels

Konrad-Adenauer-Ufer III, (172 b.)
Siegesstrasse 5A, Deutz; tel. 81 47 11 (338 b.)
An der Schanz 14, Reihl; tel. 76, 70, 81 (366 b.)

An international membership card, issued by a national Youth Hostel Association, is required. During the main holiday season the hostels get very full so booking in advance is recommended. Further information can be obtained from:
German Youth Hostel Association
(Deutsches Jugendherbergswerk),
D-4930 Detmold, PO Box 220,
Bülowstrasse 26.